More Beaded Pu

Lessons in
Knitting Techniques

Nancy Seven VanDerPuy

Schiffer Publishing Ltd

4880 Lower Valley Road, Atglen, Pennsylvania 19310

Dedication

To my dad, Ray Seven –
the wisest man I know.

Acknowledgements

I am grateful to a wonderful, creative God, who has made me in his image, giving me the ability to imagine and make beautiful things. He's also given me a supportive family of a husband and my two sons, who love me and, while they can't understand my passion for beads, they married two wonderful women who can.

I'm grateful to my sisters who help with my web site, at demonstrations, at art fairs, and also give me good feedback. My son, Tom, is the talented photographer who took most of the pictures for this book. Thanks to Sue Ann Bishop for letting me use a picture of one of her many beautiful beaded knit purses, and my friend Jodi Dulmes is always an encouragement and helper in my beading quest.

Thanks to my Dutch friends Herma Kattekamp-Remmerts and Tineke Nieuwenhuyse-Taal, whom I've only met online, for giving me much advice, help, and patterns in the technique of old Dutch bead knitting.

I appreciate Mevrouw van Velzen and Kathy Burch giving me permission to use pictures of their stunning antique beaded purses.

Copyright © 2009 by Nancy Seven VanDerPuy
Library of Congress Control Number: 2008938226

Designed by Stephanie Daugherty
Type set in Adobe Jenson/NewBskvll BT/NewsGoth BT/Smudger LET

ISBN: 978-0-7643-3172-5
Printed in China

Other Schiffer Books by Nancy Seven VanDerPuy:

Knitting Beaded Purses, A Complete Guide to Creating Your Own
978-0-7643-2870-1, $16.95

Other Schiffer Books on Related Subjects:

Beads & Agate Jewelry to Create Yourself
978-0-7643-2998-2, $14.99

Bead Crochet Jewelry, Tools, Tips, & 15 Beautiful Projects
0-7643-2023-8, $18.95

Beading Necklaces
0-88740-735-8, $12.95

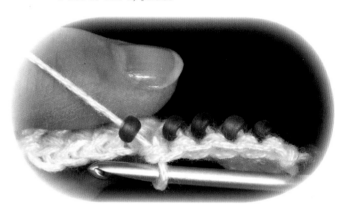

Contents

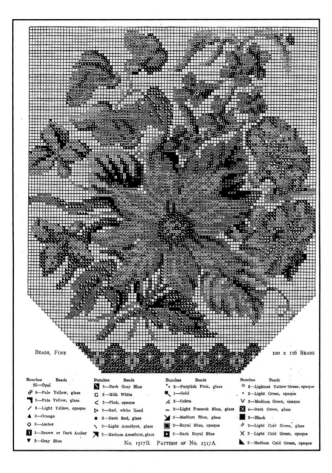

Introduction

For the last ten years I have been consumed by Bead Knitting. My passion started when I volunteered at the Sheboygan County Historical Museum in Sheboygan, Wisconsin, and was able to see the museum's collection of beaded purses. Upon close examination, I discovered that most of the purses were knit. Up until that time I had been an avid knitter, but when I saw what adding beads to the knit stitches could do, I was hooked on learning more about the art. I studied the resources I could find, but they were minimal. Most notable among them were *Mary Thomas's Knitting Book* and a video called "Bead Knitting" by Victorian Video Productions. I also pored through vintage books. They were helpful but referred to materials that were hard to find and techniques that were hard to follow. And the old patterns, being in black and white failed to show the true beauty of the finished article, so were hard to visualize.

For a couple of years, I tried various techniques and patterns. By utilizing some techniques from the old way of bead knitting and combining them with some new methods, I have found a way to do bead knitting that works.

I borrow heavily from the aforementioned resources for knitting technique, but I have created my own way of designing patterns, based on an Excel spreadsheet (my secondary passion).

This way of patterning allows the artist to not only design almost any type of scene or motif, but shows a close approximation of what the finished purse will look like, in full color.

My first book, *Knitting Beaded Purses*, was targeted to beginner bead knitters. It featured seven original patterns, all inspired by vintage purses. The patterns were very similar in shape and size, but were designed to give the new bead knitter a good grasp of basic bead knitting, choosing colors, reading patterns, stringing beads, and techniques for finishing the purse with fringe, edgings, and drawstrings.

This book will move beyond "beginner" patterns and teach new techniques that will help broaden the bead knitter's experience. The techniques are not difficult but will help build up a repertoire of methods for increasing skill. Each pattern is actually a "Lesson" in a new stitch or type of design. The lessons don't build on each other, but stand alone, so that someone reading this book could start with any of the patterns and create the purse just by following the directions for that pattern. The "Lessons" covered include Increasing, Decreasing, Adding a Purse Frame, and Working with Color.

Whereas the previous book's patterns were original, yet based on antique purse designs, the patterns of this book are original, but inspired by different things. Several patterns are based on vintages purses, but others are drawn from nature, a favorite fabric pattern, or an ethnic design. I find inspiration for my purse patterns in almost anything I see. I can look through a home décor catalog and be suddenly awakened by a pattern in a rug, a Tiffany lamp or a quilt block.

Top Left: Vintage bead knitting pattern from *The Priscilla Bead Work Book* Bottom **Left:** Picture of vintage beaded bag from *The Priscilla Bead Work Book*

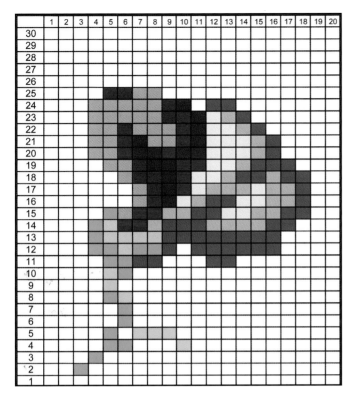

Colorized section of old beaded bag pattern from *The Priscilla Bead Work Book*.

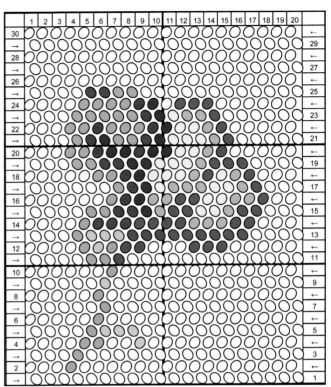

An old beaded bag pattern translated into a pattern for new bead knitting.

The dress that inspired a purse

One of my favorite motifs is plaid — any kind of plaid. It is a challenge to find correct colors for plaid designs because plaid depends on two or three main colors and combinations of the main colors. One of the patterns in this book, "The Inverness," will give you some practice in picking out colors that go together for a plaid purse. This purse was inspired by a dress that I own!

My favorite area of the world is Southwestern United States. I've made countless trips to that area and especially feel drawn to it when the wind chills in Wisconsin are twenty-five degrees below zero.

There is something different about the light, the earth, and the atmosphere in the Southwest. Not only are the landscapes inspirational, but so are the cultural arts and artifacts of New Mexico, Arizona, and Utah. I have designed many of my beaded articles with the Southwest in mind. The "Red Mesa" drew its inspiration from the Southwest.

Still, one of the greatest inspirations for my patterns is the work of our Victorian sisters. The beaded purses they created a couple of centuries ago are some of the finest artwork I have ever seen.

My favorite beaded purses are the scenic ones that depict castles, houses, and people. Many of them were done with seed beads that were so tiny that they are not even available today — nobody wants to work with them. The smallest beads I use are size 15. Some of the early purses were done with beads much smaller than those; in fact, they were about the size of a sugar crystal or grain of sand. The technique was called "Sablé," meaning "grain of sand." "These beads were so fine, at size 22 or greater (possibly size 30), needles could not pass through their center holes."[1]

This is just one of many Southwest scenes that inspire me.

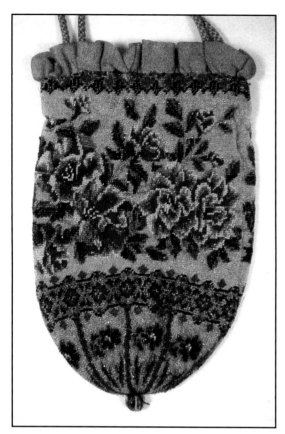

A vintage Dutch beaded purse. *Courtesy of Sietske van Velzen, photography by Rino Kattekamp.*

A vintage scenic purse. *Courtesy of Kathy Burch, Tri-State Antique Center, photography by Kathy Burch.*

Near Left: Tiny beads used in vintage beaded purses, probably size 24 or smaller, as compared to size 11 seed beads on the left. Antique beads courtesy of Jodi Dulmes.

Below: "Where your treasure is, there your heart will be also."

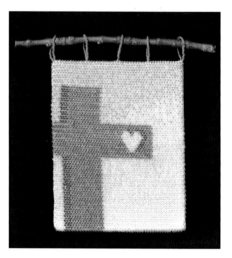

I have even found inspiration for my designs from my faith. I am an avid student of the Bible and have claimed Luke 12:33 & 34 as "mine": *Provide purses for yourselves that will not wear out, a treasure in heaven that will never fail…for where your treasure is, there your heart will be also.*

All of the directions for the purses in this book are based on the assumption that you know how to knit. If you do not, I have included a brief tutorial in *Chapter Twelve*. There are also many fine Internet sites that teach basic knitting. It's important to become quite familiar with knitting before you tackle the tiny needles that bead knitting requires. Even if you are a knitter, practice with size 0000 needles and size 8 Perle cotton before knitting a purse. Once you feel comfortable with the needles, add beads. From there, the sky is the limit. I would love to talk to you and hear how you are doing with your bead knitting. Please feel free to call or e-mail me to discuss your bead knitting successes, questions and even your failures. Believe me when I say I had more failures than successes in my first couple of bead-knitting years. I want to help you be victorious!

Abbreviations

Knitting

K – knit
P – purl
St – stitch
YO – yarn over
Inc – increase
Dec – decrease
Beg – beginning
Sl – slip
PSSO – pass slipped stitch over

Crochet

Ch – chain
Sc – single crochet
Sl st – slip stitch
YO – yarn over
Inc - increase

Chapter 1: About Bead Knitting

Combining beads with knitting is an old craft, dating back several hundreds of years. But not all knitting with beads is created equal. Besides sewing beads onto a completed knit project, there are two different methods of placing the beads on the knit fabric, while the knitting is in progress. And between these methods, there are a couple of variations. I will discuss three basic techniques:

1. **Beaded Knitting**: A bead is placed between knit stitches
2. **Old Bead Knitting**: A bead is placed directly on a knit stitch and the knitting is done in the round.
3. **New Bead Knitting**: A bead is placed directly on the knit stitches, using a twisted form of knitting. It can be done flat or in the round.

Though I will discuss all of these methods, I use only "New Bead Knitting" for the patterns in *Chapters Three–Ten*. I am currently researching "Old Bead Knitting" because I want to keep the old technique alive and understand how our Victorian sisters did their work.

When one refers to beaded knitting or bead knitting, the object in question is usually a purse. Though other things, such as scarves, hats, and sweaters can be embellished with beads, purses have been the most commonly beaded items. Illustrations and references have been made to beaded purses as far back as the fourteenth and fifteenth century, but beaded purses based on knitting were popular in the eighteenth, nineteenth, and twentieth centuries. Antique purses were usually made with either the "Beaded Knitting" method or the "Old Bead Knitting" method. The "New Bead Knitting" technique is relatively new and was promoted in the Mary Thomas book and Alice Korach's video, "Bead Knitting."

Beaded Knitting

Using this method, one or more beads are placed between stitches. It is a fairly simple technique and can result in beautiful, heavy beadwork. The thread color is an integral part of the piece because much of it will show in the work. The beads show on both sides of the piece. Varying the number of beads between stitches can result in a wavy or swag-like appearance.

Usually, only one color of bead is used in beaded knitting; a purse can have a uniform look by using a like-color thread and bead, or a nice contrast can be made between the thread color and the bead color. This method is used for necklace purses and larger purses. A large purse made with this method must be lined, since an opening in the knit fabric results by placing a number of beads between stitches. Below are instructions for making a simple beaded knit project — a Christmas Ornament. For this project you will need to know how to do a basic knit stitch (*see Chapter Twelve*).

 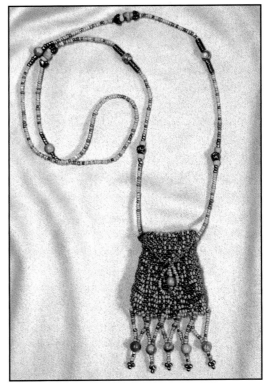

Left: A beaded-knit purse, made by Sue Ann Bishop, of Victorian Purses by Sue. *Photography by Sue Ann Bishop.* **Right:** A beaded-knit purse created by the author.

A Beaded-Knit Christmas Ornament

Materials

    2 size 0000 steel knitting needles
    20 yards of Size 8 Perle Cotton – green
    4 strands of Size 11 seed beads – white
    Various decorative beads
    Small charm (optional)
    Tapestry Needle
    Big Eye Needle

Directions

• Beads from the strands must be transferred to the Perle Cotton. Gently separate one strand from the hank. Tie a slipknot in one end of it and slip it over the end of the Perle Cotton ball. Tighten around the Perle Cotton, but don't pull so tight as to make a knot. Slide beads from strand to Perle Cotton. Thread three strands of beads onto the Perle Cotton. If you don't have strands, beads can be strung onto the Perle Cotton with a Big Eye Needle. Slide beads down the Perle Cotton for several yards; wrap around a folded rag to keep beads from becoming tangled.

• Cast on 12 stitches and knit one row.

• The rest of the bag is worked by knitting 2 stitches for the border. Slide the appropriate number of beads up to needle; knit 1 stitch, slide beads, knit 1 stitch, slide beads, and so on, and then ending with 2 knit stitches for the border.

• Section 1: Knit 8 rows with 1 bead between every stitch (except the 2 border stitches on each side). There should be nine beads in the row.

• Section 2: Knit 8 rows with 2 beads, 1 bead, 2 beads, 1 bead, and continuing that way across the row.

• Section 3: Knit 8 rows with 3 beads, 1 bead, 3 beads, 1 bead, and continuing that way across the row.

• Section 4: Knit 20 rows with 4 beads, 1 bead, 4 beads, 1 bead, and continuing that way across the row.

• Repeat Section 3.

• Repeat Section 2.

• Repeat Section 1.

• Knit one row without beads, and bind off.

• Determine which side will be the inside and weave in loose threads to the inside.

• Make a chain. Cut about 2 ½' of Perle Cotton. Thread a Big Eye Needle to the center of strand (strand is doubled). String one decorative bead and place it about 8" from the end of the strand. Thread the rest of the chain, using decorative beads and white beads to your liking; end with a decorative bead to match the first one. Total length of the chain should be about 9".

• Make fringe, if desired, before sewing up the bag. Use Nymo Size D and various beads, to your liking.

• Cut the Big Eye Needle off the chain thread and thread a Tapestry Needle onto it. Fold bag inside out (tucking in fringe if you have made fringe). Sew both side seams with the ends of the chain, from the top of the bag to the bottom. Knot and secure loose ends.

• Gently turn bag right side out. Decorate with charm if desired.

Your first beaded-knitting project!

This project will give you a good feel for working with tiny needles and knitting with beads. Knitting a small beaded-knit project like this is good preparation for bead knitting. Congratulations! You are ready to learn to Bead Knit.

Bead Knitting

The development of this method allowed the bead knitter to use many different colors. Mary Thomas described it as, "...work so fine, and patterns so realistic in colour, as to resemble miniature paintings."[2] Bead knitting is more difficult to master for two reasons: Each bead must be pre-strung on the knitting thread according to a grid, and the stitch requires a little more dexterity to get the bead on the stitch (described in detail in *Chapter Two*). In the first couple centuries of beaded purses, the "old" technique was used; the "new" technique is literally a "twist" on the old stitch.

Old Bead Knitting

Though the technique varied from country to country and even from knitter to knitter, the general method was that the purse was knitted on 4 or 5 double pointed needles, in the round.

Each row was knit and the knit stitch was accomplished by inserting the needle into the back leg of the stitch, the yarn was brought around the needle counter-clockwise, the bead pushed through the stitch to the front of the work. A pattern was constructed on a grid of squares, making them fairly easy to design. Any cross-stitch pattern could also be used, as it was based on the same square grid. This "old" method was easier than "new" bead knitting in that only one stitch type was used, but it had a big disadvantage: the finished knit piece tended to bias or skew to the left because all the beads lean that way. A purse done in this manner can be blocked.

The author made the purse featured in the pictures with a pattern taken from *Classic Beaded Purse Patterns*, a book by E. deJong-Kramer.

> **Tip:** Blocking is accomplished by wetting the purse and pinning it down on a towel placed on carpet or on a board, to the desired dimensions. It results in varying degrees of success — sometimes the purse eventually returns to its "skewed" state.

Old bead knit work in progress.

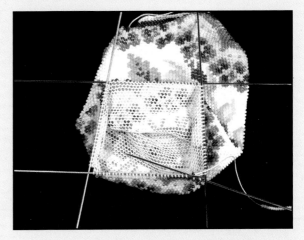

Old bead knit work – knitting on 5 needles.

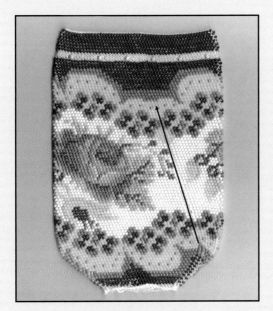

Purse made with Old Bead Knit technique, showing bias. Arrow shows actual side of purse.

Purse made with Old Bead Knit technique, after blocking.

New Bead Knitting

New Bead Knitting is a little more complicated than either of the previous methods and can, therefore, be a challenge. But the end result is a piece of art! It varies from Beaded Knitting in all the same ways that "Old Bead Knitting" varies, but it adds a new element: the Twisted Knit Stitch. I will describe it in detail in *Chapter Two*, but basically, it alternates one row of regular knitting (or purling) with one row of twisted knitting, which, in effect, turns every other row of beads to the right, eliminating the bias of old bead knitting. It can be done in either round or flat knitting. I do both kinds of bead knitting but I use this method for all the patterns in this book because it makes for a neater looking end product and eliminates the need to block the purse.

The patterns for New Bead Knitting differ from square grid patterns in that the grid must show the "offset" angle of the beads as they lay on the knitted fabric, i.e. one row of beads leans to the right, one row leans to the left. The grid resembles the way bricks lay, unlike straight squares. Thus, it is difficult to use a counted-cross stitch pattern for bead knitting — the resulting picture will be distorted. Using a brick-stitch bead pattern is a little better but the finished product is also off, in that beads in brick stitch lay horizontally, whereas beads in bead knitting lay at Northwest to Southeast or Northeast to Southwest angles.

For my patterns I've made an Excel spreadsheet studded with ovals that represent beads. I begin creating a new pattern by printing out a blank grid. Using a pencil, I roughly draw the design.

I may use colored pencils to start giving it color. Then I move back to my computer to input color into the beads. Using this method gives me a very close approximation of what the finished purse will look like.

The chart below may help you understand the different methods of knitting with beads. If you find that Bead Knitting is too difficult to begin with, start with a Beaded Knitting project. Try the sample above or find one of many free patterns on the Internet (Google "beaded knitting").

I hope that you will give bead knitting a try. The next chapter will get into more detail about how to do the art and will be followed by the pattern basics in *Chapter Three* and, starting with *Chapter Four*, "lessons" that will introduce

new techniques. By the end of the book, you may be designing your own purse! As you learn, remember that our Victorian sisters developed this craft — without the help of computers, bright lights, or #2.75 reading glasses. So there's no reason why you can't do it too.

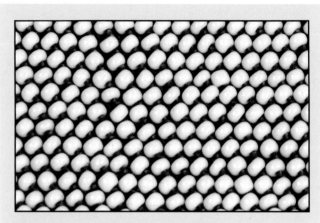

The angle of beads in Old Bead Knitting..

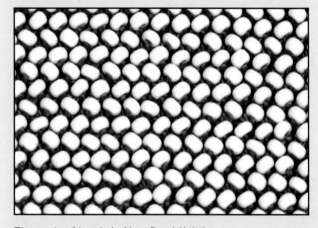

The angle of beads in New Bead Knitting.

The beginnings of a new purse pattern.

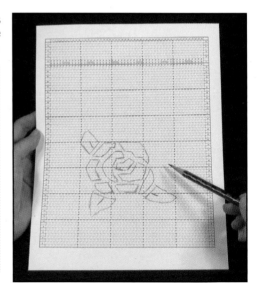

Characteristic:	Beaded Knitting	Old Bead Knitting	New Bead Knitting
Difficulty	Easiest	Harder	Hardest
Bead Placement	Between stitches	On the stitches	On the stitches
# of colors used	One	Many	Many
Stitches Used	Knit	Knit & Purl	Knit & Purl
Time	Less	More	Most
Stringing the Beads	From a Hank	One by One	One by One
Key Advantage	Heavy, nice feel	Detailed Look	Detailed Look
Key Disadvantage	One Color	Fabric tends to bias	Most difficult
Chart Layout	None	Squares	Offset; like bricks
% of Knitters that have the ability	Many	Handful	Very Few

Chapter 2: Bead Knitting Techniques

Materials

Beads

This is the MOST IMPORTANT part of your purse. When I go to a store to buy beads for a purse, I have a particular color and size in mind. It should theoretically take me about five minutes to make my purchase. But, I have rarely gotten out of a bead store in under thirty minutes. The fact is I can't ignore a single bead. I used to think I alone had an illness until I started researching the history of beads and found that there are people in all cultures, at all times that are as sick as me.

There are very few, if any, groups of people on earth who have not made beads of some sort. Not all beads were used for adornment. Earliest uses were for trade, religious ceremony and to indicate status. Beads are so common and varied, that we can tell a lot about a culture by studying its beads. "Beads so often mirror the culture of which they are a part that they tell us a great deal about the social, political, economic, and religious lives of the people who have made and worn them," says Lois Sherr Dubin in her book, *The History of Beads*.[3]

So, if the most common type of bead in the United States is a seed bead, what does that say about America? I hope future anthropologists will say of us bead workers, that we were an inventive and creative lot, striving to reach across cultures and generations to connect to our many heritages, but I'm afraid that they're just going to say we were obsessed.

There has been a beading revival in the last few years in America. Bead stores have popped up in almost every city, classes are being taught in record numbers, and beading parties are a common event for everyone from Girl Scout troops to Red Hat Societies.

Today's bead workers are making such varied items, but most projects have a common denominator —

> **Tip:** According to the American Heritage Dictionary, a bead is, "a small, ball-shaped piece of material pierced for stringing or threading." And a seed bead is a mass-produced small bead made by slicing glass tubes into uniform pieces, ranging in size from less than a millimeter to several millimeters (my definition).

the seed bead. It's the standard for most jewelry, the background for bead art, and it's the basis for beaded purses.

All of the purses in this book are constructed of either size 11 or size 15 seed beads. Several of the projects feature focal or decorative beads as embellishments but the basic building block of the bags is seed beads.

Seed beads come in such a wide variety of finishes, colors and shapes that choices are nearly infinite. For that reason, I have not given specific bead choices in my patterns. I have indicated the colors that I have used, but don't feel bound to a specific bead. Also, while local and online bead stores usually carry a wide variety of seed beads, they may not have the exact bead that I used. Feel free to substitute.

Also, don't be daunted by the huge selection of seed beads. Find the types you like best and seek those out. You may go into a store searching for a red bead and be confronted by a red matte bead, a red opaque bead, a red transparent bead, or a red rainbow mix. Usually, a purse has a better overall look if the same type of bead is used throughout, for example, if all matte beads are used, but for some purses, a mix of bead types is useful. On the Waterford purse (Chapter Eight), I've used different types of beads to make water and land stand out. The water beads shimmer more while the land beads are matte. Below is a chart that will help you understand the different types of finish on seed beads.

One of my bead drawers. At least I have them organized by color.

Bead Type	Characteristic
Transparent	Bead glass is transparent, usually shiny
Opaque	Solid color; ranges from shiny to dull
Rainbow/Iris	Finish has several colors or highlights
Pearl	Pearl-like look
Luster	Softly reflective, not shiny
Matte	Dull and smooth
Lined	Hole is lined with color
Ceylon	Pearl-like look
Metallic	Gold, Silver or Coppery look

The most common sources of seed beads today are Czechoslovakia and Japan. Most bead stores carry both types. Czech beads usually come on a hank; Japanese beads come in tubes or boxes.

Any of the purses in this book can be made in different colors. Experiment with different color mixes. One of my

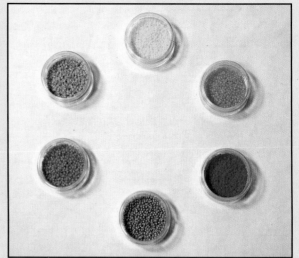

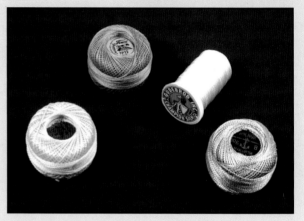

Clockwise from Top: Czech (hanks) and Japanese (tubes) seed beads. A basic color wheel. Thread that can be used for bead knitting.

favorite bead stores, Eclectica, in Brookfield, Wisconsin, has hundreds of hanks hanging on a wall. I love to hold hanks together to see how the colors flow together. If you know anything about color theory, you will understand why some colors "go" together and some clash. One of the best books on bead color mixing is Margie Deeb's *The Beader's Guide to Color*. In it are some wonderful examples of color schemes, based on the color wheel.

The simple color wheel will give you an introduction into color theory.

According to the experts, there are three primary colors (red, yellow, blue). These are pure colors and can be mixed to form secondary colors (green, orange and purple). These, in turn, can be mixed with primary colors to form tertiary colors. Color schemes are usually based on analogous colors (colors next to each other on the color wheel) or complementary colors (colors opposite each other on the wheel).

Most experts who have studied color agree that color theory is not random, but that there is some order to this. Even in nature, some color combinations create harmony and some create a feeling of chaos. To me, this indicates a "Master Designer," who planned this from the beginning, and has built into us an appreciation for beauty.

Thread

The thread HOLDS it all together.

For most projects, Perle Cotton is a good basic, and inexpensive thread. A pricier alternative is silk. For all of the purses in this book, you can use either type. Each pattern indicates what size thread to use — most of the patterns require a size 8 Perle Cotton or size F silk thread. One pattern, "The Waterford," requires thinner thread (size 12 Perle Cotton). Cotton thread is washable, durable and easy to work with. Silk is probably more durable and gives a purse a bit more of a supple feel.

The Perle Cotton I most often use is DMC. Other good alternatives are Anchor or Perle Finca by Presencia Hilaturas S. A. My favorite silk thread is Gudebrod Brothers Champion Silk. DMC Perle Cotton is widely available at craft and quilting stores; other threads are available online. I have listed a few of the sources in the "Materials" section of the Gallery.

Carefully consider what color thread you use for your purse. Although the thread will not show very much, it will be slightly visible between the beads, at the top and bottom of the purse and possibly for a drawstring. Your choice of thread color will be based on one of two situations: it can

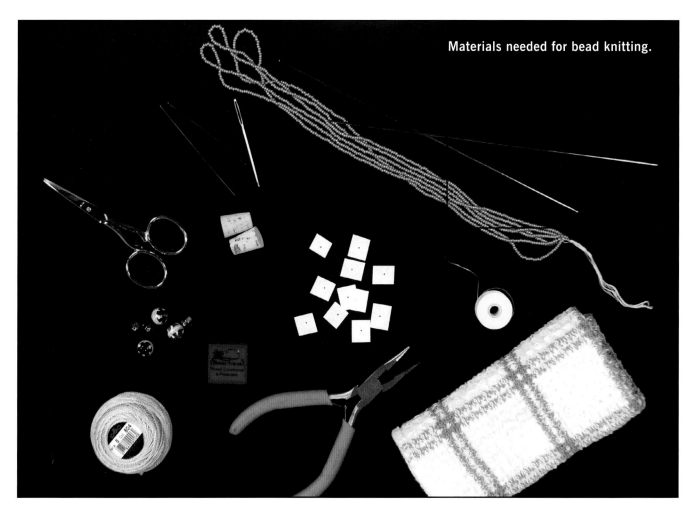

either match your main bead color, thus blending in and nearly disappearing, or it can contrast with the main color bead and give the purse an additional design element.

Other Materials

The materials listed below can be considered "tools of the trade" and are things that I generally use to complete a purse. Most of them are necessary items but I have marked a few with an asterisk (*) to indicate that they are optional. You may find good alternatives to some of these. All materials are readily available at craft stores or online.

In *Chapters Four through Ten*, I give directions for finishing each purse with a frame, drawstring, fringe, or embellishment. You may want to add or subtract from my suggestions, thus your materials might differ from mine. For example, you may want to add focal beads to a fringe, or you may want to line a purse with ultra suede instead of satin. In that case, your list of materials will change.

- *Foam pad, like "Funky Foam" or "Foamies." I have found this is the best surface for threading beads. I use a 9" x 12" white sheet.
- Big Eye Needle (I prefer Darice "Easy Eye" Beading Needles #1144-26) for stringing beads onto thread

- Thread for stringing
- Seed beads
- Miscellaneous decorative beads for embellishment
- Scrap paper for marking bead rows as they are threaded
- Small beading pliers for breaking misshapen or extra beads
- Small scissors
- Size 0000 Knitting Needles
- *Small corks for covering sharp points of knitting needles
- Cloths, like a washcloth, for winding strung beads, to keep them neat
- Bead Spinner (if stringing many beads of the same color that are purchased in tubes rather than hanks)
- *Fabric for lining
- Nymo Thread (Size D) for fringe
- Tapestry Needle (size 22) for sewing seams
- Beading Needle (size extra fine) for fringe
- Thread Heaven
- *Large Rubber Band (for purses with a frame)

Knitting with Beads

Twisted Knitting

Sometimes it's called "Plaited Knitting" and sometimes it's called "Twisted Knitting." I like to call it the latter because it sounds funkier. Whatever you call it, it's the kind of knit stitch used in bead knitting that keeps the beads in place.

A regular knit stitch is accomplished by inserting the right needle into the front part (leg) of the stitch on the left needle, and the yarn is brought around the right needle counter-clockwise *(see Chapter Twelve for Basic Knitting Instructions)*. A bead knit stitch is just the opposite: the right needle is inserted into the back leg of the stitch and the yarn is brought around the right needle clockwise. The next row (a purl row) is done as a regular purl row is done.

The effect of doing one row twisted and one row regular is that the knit fabric is a little tighter and the beads stay on the knitted fabric better.

Right: Comparison of regular knitting and twisted knitting.

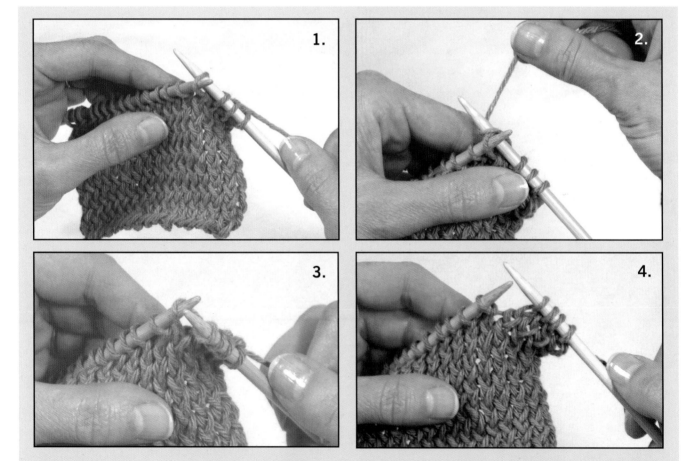

Twisted Knit Stitch: 1. *In* – right needle through back leg of stitch on left needle. **2.** *Around* – loop yarn around right needle from front to back, or clockwise. **3.** *Through* – bring right needle through the stitch on left needle. **4.** *Off* – A completed twisted knit stitch.

The Knit Stitch

If this is your first time knitting with beads, I suggest using a large size seed bead, such as a size 6, and a thin yarn, such as a sport weight cotton yarn. For this size yarn, use size 1 knitting needles (you can use regular or double pointed needles). You'll also need a foam pad and a big eye needle to string the beads.

Pour the beads onto the foam pad. Thread the needle with the yarn (leave the yarn attached to the skein). String about two hundred beads onto the yarn. Move most of the beads several feet down the yarn, toward the skein. You will need to keep sliding them down the thread as you knit, because you'll use up the yarn faster than you'll use up the beads. Remove the big eye needle.

Leaving a tail of about two feet, cast on twenty-four stitches loosely. Purl one row loosely. In preparation for knitting the next row with beads, move a few beads up to within a few inches of your knitting needles. Knit the first two stitches in a twisted knit stitch (knit into the back "leg" of the stitch, yarn over needle clockwise) for the selvage edge. Knit the next twenty stitches with beads as shown in the pictures. Knit the last two stitches in twisted knit without beads.

Twisted Knit Stitch with Beads: 1. *In* – insert needle through back leg of the stitch, to back of work. 2. *Up* – slide a bead up to within about a half inch of needles. 3. *Around* – loop yarn around needle from front to back, forcing bead between needles. 4. *Through* – with your left forefinger, pop bead between needles and to the front of work. 5. *Off* – pull completed stitch off left needle.

A bead spinner.

TIP: If you must string many beads of the same color but can't find them on hanks, you can use a Bead Spinner. This amazing tool spins the beads right onto your thread. It's mysterious. I haven't quite figured it out.

1.

2.

3.

4.

5.

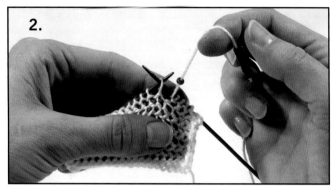

The Purl Stitch

For the purl row, purl the first 2 stitches without beads and then purl 20 stitches with beads as shown in the steps below. Purl the last two stitches without beads.

Continue these two rows until you have made a sample swatch of about twenty rows of beads. This will give you a good idea of how the rows and stitches should look and will make you comfortable with the technique. If you'd like to try progressively smaller beads and needles, see the chart below.

Bead Size	Thread Size	Needle Size
6	Sport Weight	1
8	#5 Perle Cotton	0
11	#8 Perle Cotton	0000
15	#12 Perle Cotton	000000

This chart shows which size beads, thread, and needles work best together. In bead knitting, it's easiest to use thread that is thick enough to hold the beads in place without them sliding freely, yet they can still be pushed along the thread. However, using a thinner thread gives a purse a suppler feel and the thread is less visible. Experiment with different size threads, beads and needles to see what appeals to you.

Comparison of bead knitting using bead and thread combinations in chart.

Left Column: Purl Stitch with Beads: 1. *In* – insert needle through front leg of stitch, to front of work. **2. *Up* –** slide a bead up to within about a half inch of needles. **3. *Around* –** loop yarn around needle from back to front, forcing bead between needles. **4. *Through* –** with your left thumb, pop bead between needles and to the right side of work. **5. *Off* –** pull completed stitch off left needle.

Correcting Errors

As you learn bead knitting, and even after you become an expert, you will make mistakes in stringing the beads. You will string too many, too few, or you'll string the wrong color. Sometimes a bead will be misshapen and have to be removed. When this happens, you'll have to correct the error before proceeding. There are a couple of ways to correct errors. If your error is only a row or two back, you can un-knit or un-purl up to the point of the error, correct it, and then continue forward. The illustrations below show how to un-knit or un-purl.

If you must remove one or two beads, they can be carefully crushed with a bead pliers, but be sure not to cut into the thread. If you must add beads, you will have to cut the thread and correct the bead sequence.

If you don't catch an error until several more rows have been completed, you can tear out bead knitting row by row. Insert a free needle into every stitch in a row below the error. Remove your working needle from your last finished row. Carefully pull each bead stitch out, row

A free needle is inserted into each stitch of a row, several rows below the mistake.

after row, until you come to the free needle. Bead stitches are more difficult to rip out than regular knitting so take care to manipulate the beads through the stitches as you pull.

Un-Knit Stitch – 1. slip tip of left needle into the stitch one row below, from behind. 2. Slide the stitch off the right needle and pull the stitch out with your right hand. 3. A completed Un-Knit Stitch.

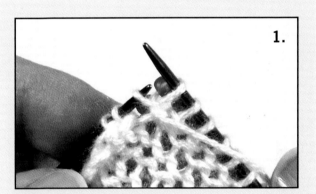

Un-Purl Stitch – 1. slip tip of left needle into the stitch one row below, from behind. 2. Slide the stitch off the right needle and pull the stitch out with your right hand. 3. A completed Un-Purl Stitch.

Matress Stitch: 1. Catch the horizontal bar of the knit stitch immediately next to the bead on the left-hand piece. 2. Catch the horizontal bar of the knit stitch immediately next to the bead on the right-hand piece. 3. Mattress Stitch in progress.

Sewing Seams

You'll use the Mattress Stitch to sew up the sides and bottom of your purse. You can use the same thread used in the purse or you can use Nymo size D. *(For more information on the Mattress Stitch, see Chapter Twelve.)*

Crochet with Beads

Bead crochet is easier than bead knitting, in that beads are just pushed up to a stitch and then the stitch is completed; the bead doesn't go through a stitch. There are a couple of ways to accomplish a bead crochet stitch. The directions that follow show how to do bead crochet for "The Baltimore" purse in *Chapter Ten*. To practice bead crochet, use size 6 beads, a sport weight yarn and a size C or D crochet hook.

Start a practice piece of bead crochet with a chain 10, turn, and single crochet back *(see Chapter Twelve for Crochet Basics)*. Now start adding beads. Insert hook into next single crochet, slide a bead up to stitching, yarn over, and pull loop through single crochet. Yarn Over and pull through the two loops — one bead single crochet completed. Continue with the rest of the single crochet in the row.

In bead crocheting, the beads go to the side of the fabric away from you. If you continue to practice on this piece, every other row of beads will be on opposite sides of your work. Most bead crochet is done in the round (as in "The Baltimore") so all the beads are on the same side of the work.

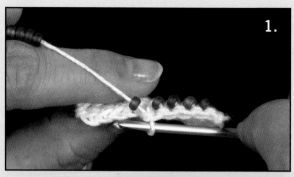

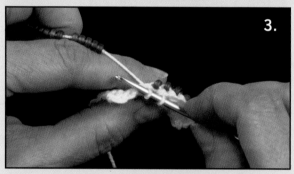

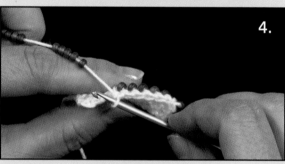

Crocheting with Beads: 1. Slide bead up to stitching. 2. Yarn Over the hook. 3. Pull up loop. 4. Yarn Over and pull through two loops – completed single crochet stitch with bead.

TIP: In another method of crochet with beads, insert the hook in single crochet in row below, yarn over, slide bead up to stitch, yarn over, and draw through the two loops. This slight difference creates a firmer, tighter fabric. For "The Baltimore" purse you want a looser fabric so it drapes well at the bottom of the purse.

Chapter 3: Pattern Basics

Reading a Chart

All of the patterns in this book are in the form of a grid (chart). Each bead must be strung in order by following the rows on the grid. The rows are numbered along the sides of the chart — odd row numbers on the right represent knit rows and even row numbers on the left represent purl rows. Numbers on the top just indicate how many beads are in each row. Arrows show from which way you will be stringing the beads. Heavy lines on the chart mark every 10 rows or 10 beads across. I've indicated groups of 10 because it makes counting beads easier. The beads on the chart lay in the same orientation that they will lay on a completed purse so the chart gives a close representation of what the purse will look like.

Always string a purse from the top row down. The last bead strung is the first bead knit. If a purse is large, you may want to string the bottom half first, start knitting it, then string the top half. This prevents the thread from becoming too worn out from too many beads sliding over it, and it makes the long string of beads more manageable.

Tip: The grid only shows beaded stitches. Always knit two extra stitches at the beginning and end of the row for a selvage edge. Each pattern's directions will tell you how many stitches to cast on. Always purl one row after casting on the first stitches. The first row with beads is a knit row.

Sample pattern.

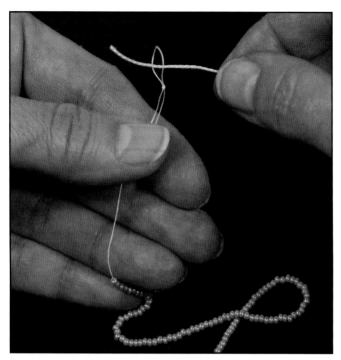

Stringing the Beads

A purse of one color is, of course, easier to make than a multi-color purse. If your beads are on hanks, you must slide the beads from the hank threads to your knitting thread. If your beads are in tubes, they can be strung onto the knitting thread with a bead spinner.

To slide beads from a hank to your thread, carefully separate one strand of beads from the rest of the hank. Tie the strand onto your thread with a slipknot. Slide the beads carefully from the hank thread to your knitting thread.

Since the patterns in this book use many colors, you will not be able to use this technique. However, for "The Pasadena" pattern, the top half of the purse (above the rose) could be strung using this method.

Top Left: Sliding beads from a hank to the working thread.

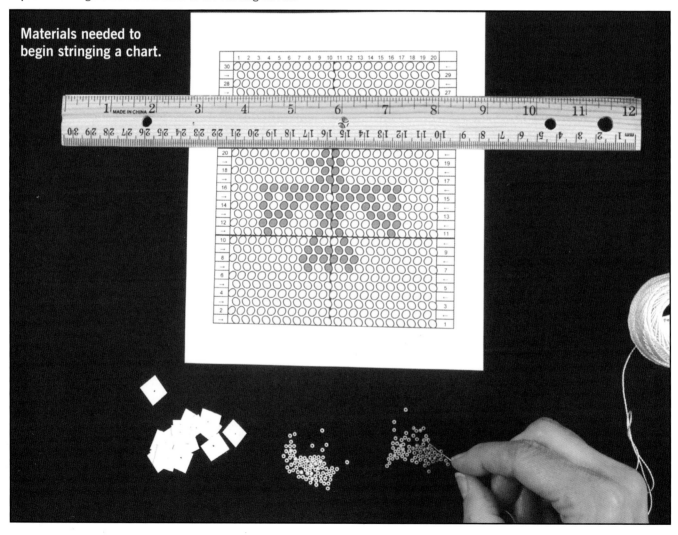

Materials needed to begin stringing a chart.

To begin stringing a pattern, you will need these materials:

- Size 11 seed beads, in all colors needed for pattern
- Size 8 or 12 Cotton Perle (depending on the pattern)
- Big Eye Needle
- Scrap paper cut into small squares
- Wash cloth or rag
- Ruler or other straight edge
- Foam pad

With materials laid out on your foam pad and needle threaded with the Perle Cotton, begin stringing the beads. Leave the thread attached to the ball since you will be pushing the beads down many yards of thread as you string. You may want to unroll the ball for 30-40 feet and push the first beads all the way down, then space out the rest of the beads along the length.

It helps to follow the chart if you lay the ruler above the row you are working on and use it as a guide. Begin stringing at the top of the chart, on the side with the arrow. After stringing one row, slide the ruler down and string the next row, from the arrow. Continue this way down through the entire chart.

After the rows of beads are strung, roll the ball of Perle Cotton in a rag and continue rolling the string of beads around the rag. This will keep your long string of beads from getting tangled.

As per the bead knitting instructions in *Chapter Two*, you will be working all the purses in twisted knitting, that is, purl rows are worked in the usual manner, but knit stitches are worked by inserting the right needle into the back of the stitch, and the yarn is brought around the needle clockwise.

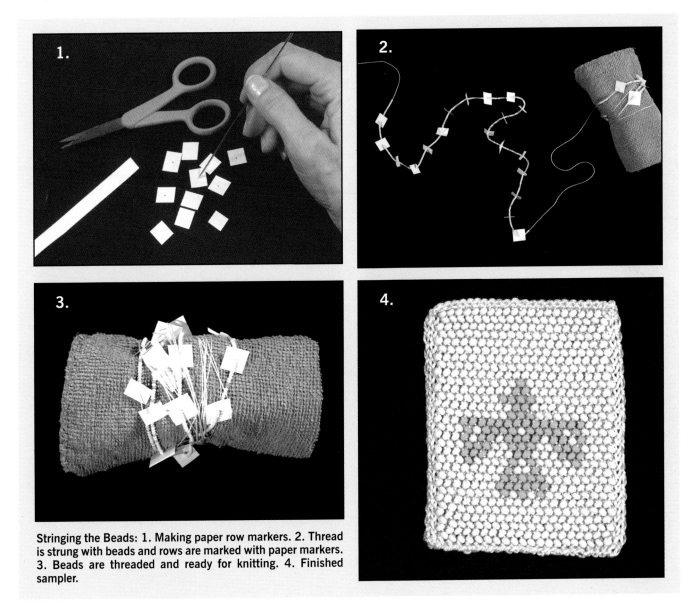

Stringing the Beads: 1. Making paper row markers. **2.** Thread is strung with beads and rows are marked with paper markers. **3.** Beads are threaded and ready for knitting. **4.** Finished sampler.

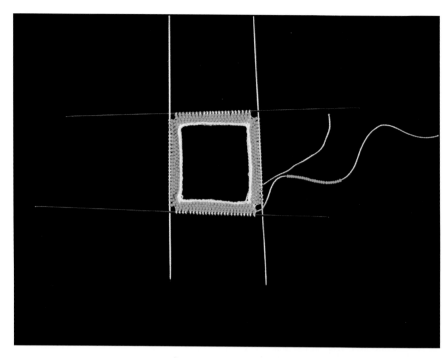

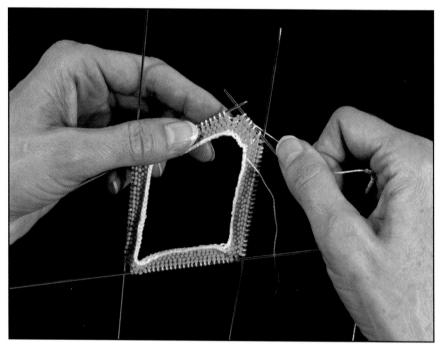

All of the purses in this book are made by knitting each side separately and sewing them together. Most of them can also be made in the round. If you would like to knit them in the round, cast on the number of stitches needed (omit the 2 stitches required for the selvedge edge). The purse must still be knit in twisted knitting, but this is accomplished in circular knitting by alternating rows between a twisted knit row (inserting the right needle into the back of the stitch and bringing the yarn around clockwise), and a regular knit row (inserting the needle into the front of the stitch and bringing the yarn around counter-clockwise).

I have not given specific bead colors for any of the patterns. Bead colors vary so much and bead color numbers can be different from one vendor to the next. Be creative in choosing colors. Use the pictures as a guideline but feel free to experiment with bead color and bead finish. I generally prefer matte or luster finish beads, but sometime a shiny bead can create a fabulous look. Hematite beads are my favorite type and they have a very shiny, showy finish.

The following patterns are presented as lessons. In my first book, *Knitting Beaded Purses*, the patterns were basically the same type of construction, with different designs. It was written as an introduction to bead knitting and was intended to give the knitter good practice for making beaded purses. The following patterns will each introduce one new technique. Some are quite simple but some are a little more challenging. Start with the following pattern, which introduces increasing in bead knitting. It's not a difficult thing and can produce a nicely rounded drawstring purse.

All patterns list materials that are part of the purse. General materials used in construction of the purses are listed in *Chapter Two*.

Top: Knitting in the round – stitches divided onto four needles. **Above:** Knitting in the round in progress.

Chapter 4: Lesson One –Increasing
The Pasadena

The Pasadena

This purse style was very popular in the 1800s and was called a Réticule. Réticule is a French word derived from the Latin word for "net." It was used to carry a lady's toiletries and was usually beaded, but might also have been embroidered or crocheted. It has a simple design and is not hard to string. The bottom half of the purse (with the rose) must be strung according to the chart, but the top part can be strung by transferring hanks to your knitting thread, or if you have loose beads, they can be strung with a bead spinner.

Materials

· Size 11 seed beads, pink and off-white
· Size 8 Perle Cotton, off-white
· Nymo Size D, off-white
· Decorative Beads
· Fabric for lining (optional)
· Satin Cord

> TIP: In bead knitting, an increase is made in the row previous to where you add the extra bead. You will increase 1 stitch in the first row, but you won't add the extra bead until the next row.

Instructions

• String rows 45–1; cast on 29 stitches; and purl one row.

• Next row: Knit one increase in first stitch, knit 1 (so there are now 3 stitches without beads at beginning of row), knit 25 stitches with beads, knit 2.

• Next row: Purl one increase in first stitch, purl 1 (so there are now 3 stitches without beads at beginning of row), purl 26 stitches with beads, purl 2

• Continue in this way, increasing 1 stitch at beginning of each row through row 30. On row 31, don't increase; keep knitting straight with beads (and 2 stitches without beads on each side for selvedge edge) until row 45 is completed.

• String the rest of the beads for rows 45-86 by sliding hanks of beads onto your knitting thread. You will need about 2,100 beads, or about 6 hank strands. If you are not using strands of beads, you can string the beads individually or use a bead spinner.

• Finish knitting the purse up to row 75.

• Row 76: Purl one row without beads

• Row 77: Knit one row in western knitting (insert needle into front of stitch and bring yarn around counterclockwise) without beads, creating eyelets according to the pattern, remembering to count the 2 selvedge edge stitches (knit 6 at beginning and end of row, make eyelets of knit 2 together, yarn over, and 7 stitches in between eyelets).

• Row 78: Purl one row without beads.

• Continue rows 79-86 with beads.

• Bind off next row; leave a long thread for sewing seams

Make two sides of the purse. Sew side seams together with Mattress Stitch. Sew bottom seam with Mattress Stitch. Weave in any loose ends of thread on the inside of the purse. Knots can be reinforced with a tiny dot of nail polish, if desired.

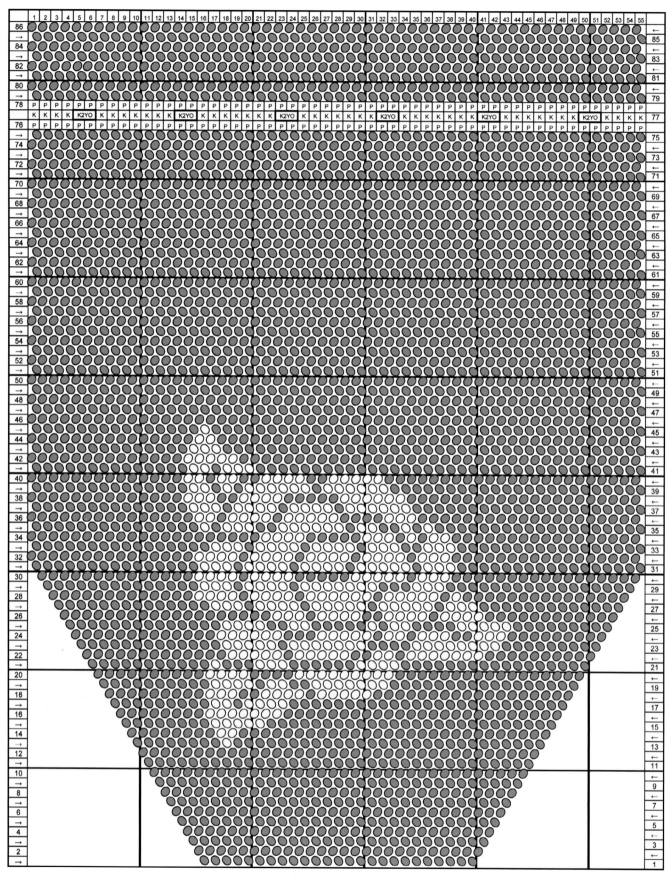

Chart for stringing "The Pasadena."

Fringe: 1. Thread 50 beads. 2. Bring new fringe behind and through previous fringe. 3. Insert needle in and out of purse bottom for next fringe. 4. Completed fringe; string 50 beads again.

Fringe – Interlocked Loop Fringe

Cut a piece of Nymo about two yards long, thread onto a beading needle. Weave Nymo into an inside seam of purse, knot it, and bring it to the outside near row 31. Thread 50 beads. Insert needle back into purse bottom less than ¼" to the left of the first fringe (creating a loop) and then back out about halfway between the legs of the loop. String another 50 beads. Bring needle behind and through previous fringe. The loops will twist together. Continue across bottom of purse, knotting thread every few loops to secure it. After last fringe, bring Nymo back inside purse, knot it, and weave the end into the side seam of purse.

For the decorative bead fringe, cut another piece of Nymo about a yard long. Weave and knot it into the inside seam and bring it to the outside of the purse at about row 1. String 20 beads, 1 small decorative bead, 3 beads, decorative bead, 10 beads, decorative bead, and 3 beads. Bring needle back through first decorative bead and up through first 20 beads, back to inside of purse. Knot the thread and weave through seam to bottom center of purse.

Decorative fringe.

TIP: It may be easier to use Nymo to sew the bottom seam of the purse, since the cast-on edges are a little denser than a side seam.

For center fringe, string 20 beads, 1 small decorative bead, 3 beads, decorative bead, big bead, decorative bead, and 3 beads. Bring needle up through big bead and all other beads back into purse. Knot and weave through seam to other bottom corner of purse. Make fringe to match first decorative fringe.

Picot Trim

Thread beading needle with about a yard of Nymo. Weave through inside seam of purse and knot near top of purse. Bring needle to outside of purse and up through a bead on last row of purse. String three beads. Bring needle back down through next bead. A picot of three beads is made. Bring needle up again through next bead in row, string three beads and go back down in next bead. Continue in this way across the top of the purse. End at side seam, weave, and knot Nymo in the inside seam.

> TIP: Condition Nymo by holding thread down on Thread Heaven and drawing the thread across. Do this a couple of times. Then run the thread between your fingers. This will condition and straighten the thread, making it easier to work with.

Right Column: Picot Trim – 1. Bring thread up through bead. 2. Bring thread down through next bead. 3. A picot of three beads.

Drawstring

Cut 2 silk or satin cords, each about 2' long. Begin stringing from the one seam side of the purse by inserting the cord into the first eyelet, out of the second one, and so on, around the whole purse, coming out the last hole. Thread the second cord in this way from the opposite side of the purse. Pull drawstrings gently until the purse top closes evenly. Make a neat knot about 7" or 8" from purse, on each drawstring, making sure the knots are even in length from the purse. If desired, string a large bead onto the ends of each cord, and knot the cord. Trim cord about 1" from the knot.

Lining

It's not necessary to line "The Pasadena." The knit fabric forms sort of a "self-lining." However, you may line it if you want to increase its durability. A pattern for lining the purse is shown. Measurements are not exact or to scale — your purse might have different dimensions, due to tighter or looser knitting. If it's easier, trace your purse onto a piece of fabric, placing the bottom of the purse on a fold of fabric. Leave enough for a ½" seam on the sides and to fold down under the eyelets. I use a good quality cotton/poly (pre-washed) or satin. Cotton is easier to take care of; satin is more elegant.

Sew ½" seams on sides. Trim seams close to sewing line. Fold top of lining down about ½" and insert lining into purse. Adjust lining to sit just below the eyelet row. Pin lining into place and sew top fold to purse.

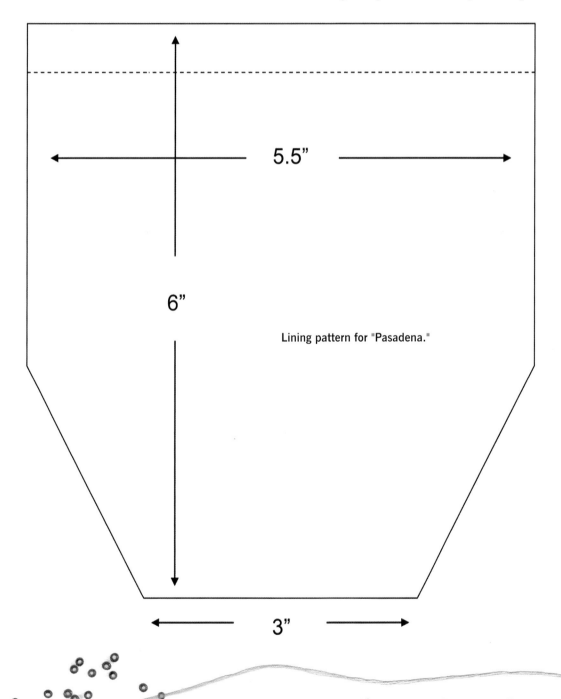

5.5"

6"

3"

Lining pattern for "Pasadena."

Chapter 5: Lesson 2 – Decreasing
The Red Mesa

The Southwestern United States is one of my favorite places in the world. I travel there frequently and always long to go back. What inspires me most is the light and landscape, but I'm always thrilled to hike in the massive rock canyons and find evidence of earlier civilizations in the form of pottery shards, arrowheads and, of course, beads! When I see these things, I feel connected to the person who made them, in the sense that we were both created in God's image. God is wonderfully imaginative and artistic and has given us a bit of that creativity. In this purse I've honored God's beautiful creation by depicting a southwestern sunset superimposed with an image similar to a Native American design, but to me, is another interpretation of God's creation (Job 12:7-10).

> **TIP:** To decrease in bead knitting, you decrease the number of beads in one row but actually make the stitch decrease in the next row.

Above: My inspiration.

The Red Mesa

Materials

· Size 11 Seed Beads — *Turquoise, Light Turquoise, Lavender, Pink, Orange, Yellow, Brown, Medium Brown, Gray, Off White, Black, Silver*
· Size 8 Perle Cotton (Off-White)
· Silver Purse Chain
· Leather or Suede Cord
· Decorative Beads or Charms that will fit over leather cord
· 2 Large Split Rings
· Magnetic Clasp
· Split Ring Tool
· Chain Cutter
· Jewelry Pliers
· Medium Interfacing
· Lining Fabric (cotton/poly, pre-washed)
· Sewing Needle and Thread (Off-White)

Instructions

• String rows 40–1 of side 1. Cast on 64 stitches. Purl one row.

• Next row: Knit 2 stitches, Knit 60 stitches with beads, knit 2 stitches

• Next row: Purl 2 stitches, purl 60 stitches with beads, purl 2 stitches

• Continue on until you finish row 40. String rows 79–41. Knit as usual. Bind off on next row. Leave a long thread for sewing seams.

Chart for stringing the front of "The Red Mesa."

- Make side two like side one, but don't bind off.

- String rows 111–80 of chart for top flap. Knit and purl rows 80, 81, and 82 as usual.

- Row 83: Knit the two selvedge stitches, knit 1 stitch without beads, knit 58 stitches with beads, knit 3 stitches without beads.

- Row 84: Purl 1, slip 1, purl 1, pass over, purl 1 without a bead, purl 56 with beads, purl 1, purl 2 together, purl 1.

- Row 85: Knit 1, slip 1, knit1, pass over, knit 1 without a bead. Knit 54 with beads, knit 1, knit 2 together, knit 1.

- Continue the last two rows, decreasing the number of beaded stitches in each row, until there are 3 beads left. Do one row without beads. Bind off.

- Sew side seams and bottom seam in Mattress Stitch. Nymo can be used for the bottom seam if desired. Reinforce knots with a tiny dot of nail polish if desired.

Chart for stringing the back of "The Red Mesa."

Chain

For this purse, the chain is meant to stabilize the side seams and the leather cord handle — it will not show. So the chain can be any type of silver purse chain. Cut two sections of chain, each measuring about an inch longer than the inside seam of the purse. From the bottom of the purse, sew the chain up along the inside seam. Cut the chain just at the top of the inside seam and attach a split ring.

Lining

To stabilize the purse, reinforce it with interfacing. Cut two pieces of interfacing about 5 x 5 ¼". Turn purse inside out and stitch interfacing to front and back of inside of purse. Turn purse right side out.

Cut a piece of lining fabric about 14 ½" x 6", tapering the top to conform to about a ½" larger than the top of the purse (your measurements might be slightly different based on your knitting tension). Fold the straight 6" end of lining

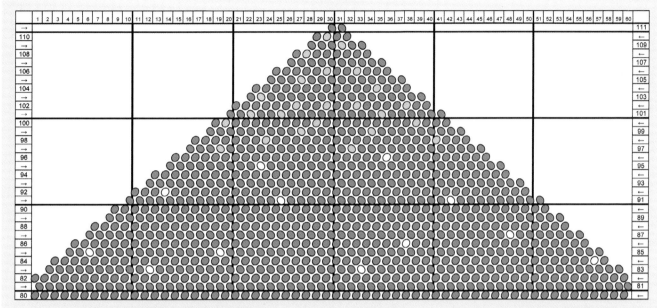

Chart for stringing the front flap of "The Red Mesa."

up about 5 ½", then fold front edge over ½". Sew side seams from bottom fold to front edge fold. Iron side seams to the back.

Hold split rings out of the way of the lining by pinning them with a safety pin outside of the purse. Insert lining into purse and sew front edge of lining to front edge of purse. Fold top flap of lining to top flap of purse, folding it over about ½" and carefully matching it to the purse flap. Leave a small gap on sides of purse for split rings.

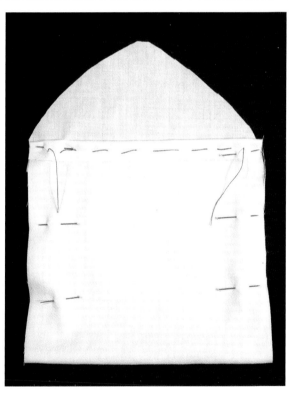

Clockwise from top: Lining for "Red Mesa," folded over. Split ring at top of chain. Close-up of "Red Mesa" handle.

Handle

Cut a piece of leather cord. If a shoulder bag is desired, cut cord about 58" long (for a shorter handle, measure desired length of handle, then add 20" for beaded side decorations). Tie cord to split rings, leaving 10" of cord hanging below split rings. Thread beads, charms, or feathers onto leather cord in desired configuration. Tie knot below beads. Cut excess cord.

Chapter Six: Lesson 3 – Old to New
The Fairhaven

A Miser Purse from the nineteenth century.

I have included a pattern for this "Miser Purse" because it's so unique in the twenty-first century, although its style was very popular in the eighteenth, nineteenth, and early twentieth centuries. It usually included two rings around the center section and coins were stored in both ends of the bag. Generally it was worn folded over a belt. It was probably called a Miser Purse because the coins were secure in the pouches, but they were hard to get to. Most Misers had the two beaded end pouches, but were plain knit in the middle with a center slit to access the coins. One side of the miser is usually rounded and one squared. My Miser Purse is the same style as many Misers of a couple hundred years ago, but I've updated the design and colors.

Materials

- · Size 11 Seed Beads — *Cream, Beige, Medium Brown, Dark Brown, Black*
- · Size 8 Perle Cotton – Ecru
- · Decorative Beads
- · Nymo Size D – Off White

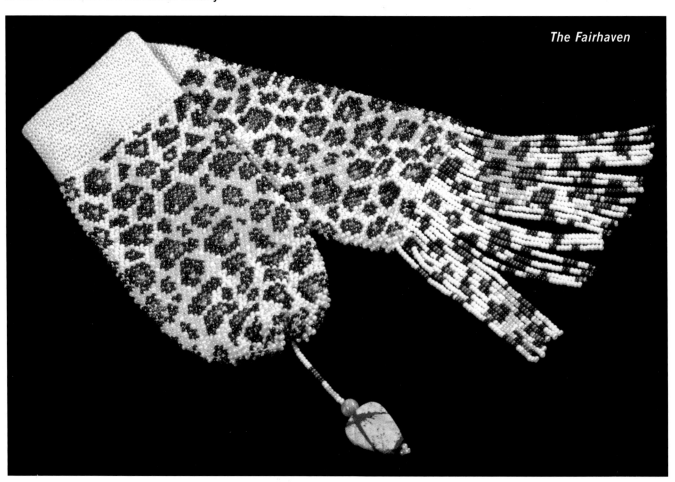

The Fairhaven

The opening at the back of "The Fairhaven."

Instructions

- String rows 30–1. Cast on 64 stitches and purl one row.

- Next row: Knit 2 stitches, knit 60 stitches with beads, knit 2 stitches.

- Next row: Purl 2 stitches, purl 60 stitches with beads, purl 2 stitches.

- Continue with these two rows until you finish row 30. String rows 65–31. Knit rows 31–65 as above. Row 65 will be a knit row. Purl one row without beads.

- Now, knit every row (Garter Stitch) without beads for the middle section of the purse. Do this for about 3 ½". End with a wrong side row so you are starting the next section with a knit row.

- String the whole chart again, starting with rows 30–1. Knit that section, string rows 65–31, and knit that.

- Upon completion of row 65 (a knit row), don't cast off. Cut the thread, leaving a 2' tail. Thread the tail onto a yarn needle and pull the tail through all stitches on the needle. Carefully pull the tail to gather the end of the purse into a bunch and join the selvage edges. Make a couple of knots to secure the edges together. With the same tail thread, sew up this beaded section of the purse with the Mattress Stitch, knot and cut the thread at the end of the beaded section, leaving the un-beaded knit section of the purse open.

- With another 2' length of thread, sew up the other beaded section of the purse, along the selvage edges, forming the rest of the back seam. Sew the bottom edge of this second beaded section.

TIP: To make a smoother edge on the middle section (unbeaded section) of your purse, slip the first stitch of every row.

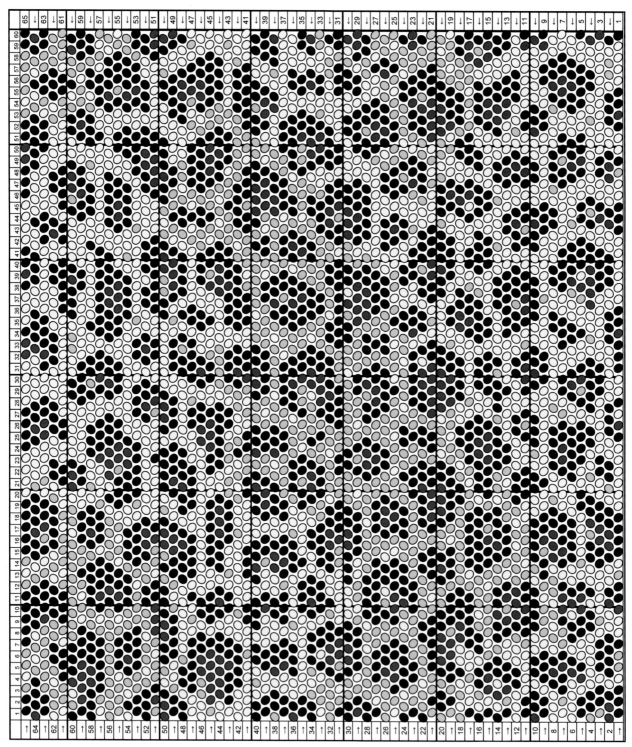

Chart for stringing "The Fairhaven."

Chapter Six: Lesson 3 – Old to New

Fringe – Straight Fringe

One end of your Miser Purse will have a gathered end, the other will have a flat end. Finish the flat end with fringe.

String about two yards of Nymo size D (Off White) on a beading needle. Condition with Thread Heaven. Run Nymo inside purse along the left inside seam (with back of purse facing you) and knot a couple of times to secure it. With the purse's back facing you, and the flat bottom seam nearest you, bring Nymo to outside of purse at lower left corner.

Read the fringe chart as columns. String the 65 beads of column 1, starting with row 1. Push beads up against the bottom of the purse. Skipping the last bead strung, run the needle up through the next 64 beads — pull snugly up against the bottom of the purse. Insert needle into bottom of purse close to first thread, then out again, roughly in line with next bead on bottom row of purse. Repeat stringing the next 65 beads (column 2, starting with row 1).

Finish all 30 fringes. Run Nymo back into the bottom of the purse, along a seam, and knot it a couple of times. If desired, finish the gathered end of the purse with one long decorative fringe, a beaded loop, or a charm.

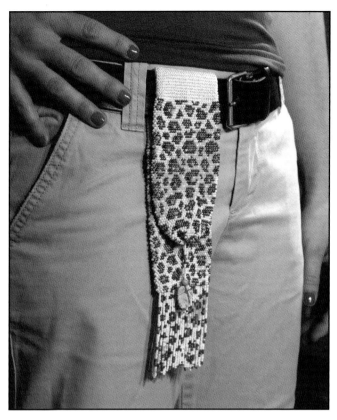

Carrying a miser purse properly.

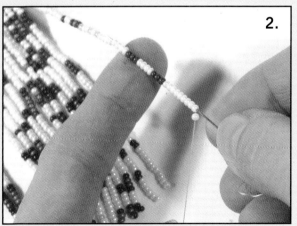

Straight Fringe: 1. String 65 beads from the fringe chart. 2. Run needle back up the column of beads.

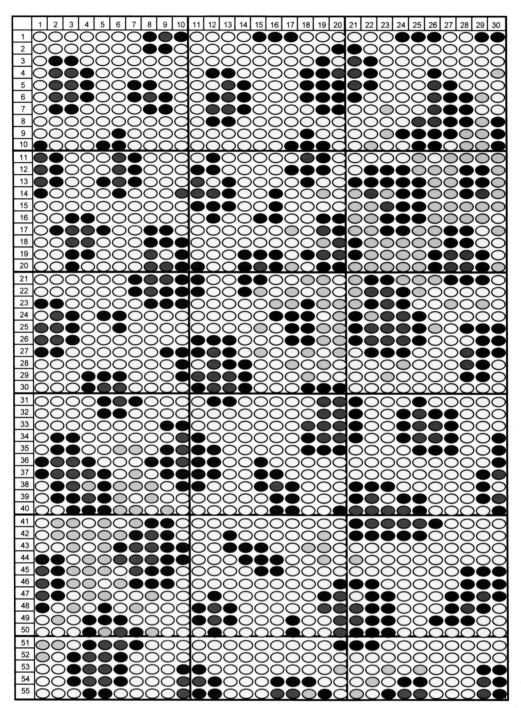

Chart for stringing fringe for "The Fairhaven."

Chapter Seven: Lesson 4 – Adding a Frame
The Chantilly

The pattern for this purse was inspired by a Tiffany Lamp. I love the geometric lines of windows, lamps, or carpets designed in the Tiffany style. The stark lines of the upper pattern of this purse are offset by the wandering vines at the bottom of the purse — a typical Tiffany design element.

A beaded purse with a frame is one of the most beautiful but difficult purses to make. Bringing the three sections together (beadwork, lining, and frame) requires patience and some hand-sewing skill. This square-framed purse is one of the easier framed purses to construct since there are no curves to negotiate, but it still takes practice and perseverance to master it.

Materials

- Size 11 seed beads — *Off White, Light Green, Medium Green, Black, Red*
- Size 8 Perle Cotton, Off White
- One 4.7" gold, square frame (like an LS87)
- Gold Purse Chain
- Chain Cutters
- 2 Split Rings
- Fabric for lining (pre-washed cotton/poly or satin)
- Sewing thread and needle, pins
- Size 7 crochet hook

Instructions

- String rows 45–1. Cast on 59 stitches (leave a long tail to sew up side seams) and purl one row without beads.

- Next row: Knit 2 stitches, knit 55 stitches with beads, knit 2 stitches.

- Next row: Purl 2 stitches, purl 55 stitches with beads, purl 2 stitches.

- Continue with these two rows until you finish knitting row 45. String rows 90–46. Work these rows as previous rows. Bind off after row 90. Make second side as the first.

- With right sides facing up, align both sides of purse, sew side seams using Mattress Stitch. Sew from bottom to top and sew only up to about row 66 (about 6 rows down from top horizontal black row of beads). This is where the frame will begin. Do not fasten off thread; leave loose in case adjustments must be made. Sew bottom seam with Perle Cotton or Nymo.

- Fringe on this purse is optional. If you'd like to put fringe on, do it before lining the purse.

The Chantilly

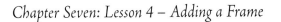

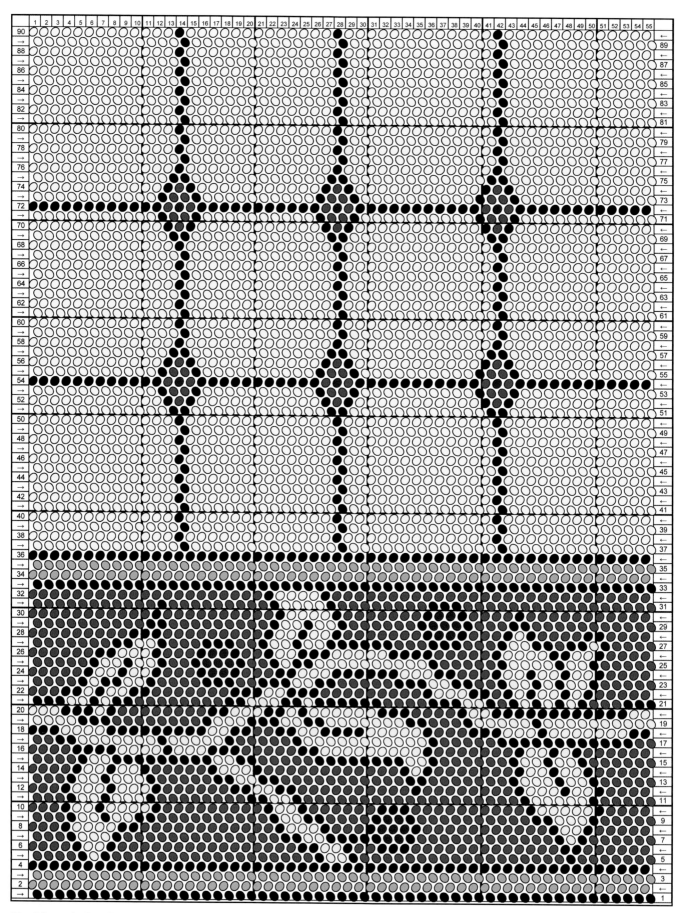

Chart for stringing "The Chantilly."

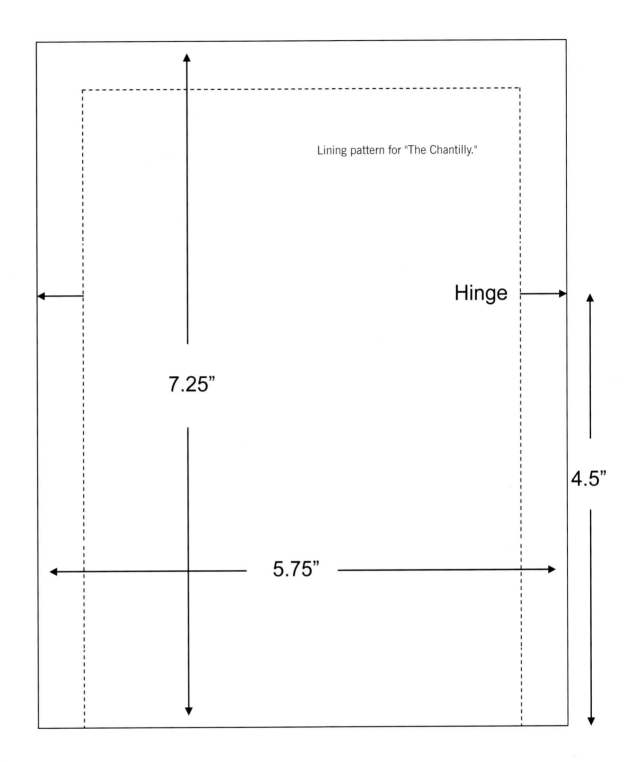

Lining pattern for "The Chantilly."

Hinge

7.25"

4.5"

5.75"

Lining

Measurements for lining are approximate because of variations in knitting tension, bead size, and frame type. I have included a lining pattern, but it may not fit every purse because of the variations.

You will need about ¼ yard of cotton, silk, satin, or any desired fabric. Fold fabric and lay bottom of purse about 1/8" below fold. Lay frame on top of purse in approximately the position it will be permanently sewn. Trace ¼" to ½" out around bottom 2/3 of purse. Mark fabric where hinge of frame lays. Trace around frame, about ¼" to ½" out from frame. Pin fabric together and cut out.

Sew side seams from bottom of purse to frame mark on both sides. Make seam about ¼" to ½". Trim seam to 1/8" to 1/4". Fit lining into purse to see if it fills the inside without being too loose or too tight.

Remove lining from purse. Fold over frame area of one side of lining about ¼" to ½". Baste. Test size of lining by fitting it into frame. It should fit into frame snugly. If not, remove basting and re-baste to fit frame. Baste other side of lining to fit frame.

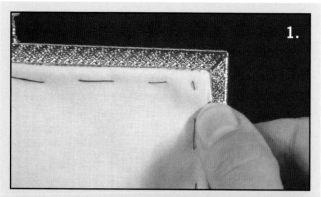

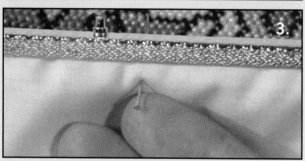

Lining the Purse: 1. Fit lining into frame to see if it fits snugly. 2. Sew lining to purse. 3. Fit and pin lining into frame. 4. Pieces of rubber band can keep pins in place. 5. Crocheted border for lining.

Put lining back inside purse. Sew basted part of lining to top of purse, using small stitches along selvedge edges of purse. Remove basting stitches.

Fit one side of the purse and lining into one side of the frame. Secure with pins in several places by poking pin from inside out through sewing holes in frame. Cut small squares of rubber band. Push over pins that are holding lining to frame. This keeps the pins in place while you sew the lining into the frame. Sew purse to frame with sewing needle and thread. Starting at one hinge side of frame, sew through holes in frame into purse and lining. It works best to come up in one hole, go down in the previous hole, up in next hole, down in previous one.

Stitches that secure frame to purse will be a little uneven and may be covered if desired. I usually crochet a border that I sew into place (instructions below). But any ribbon or decorative embellishment can be used. Measure approximate length of ribbon and pin in place (through sew holes in frame).

Crocheted Border

With a #7 hook, and Size 8 Perle Cotton (the same as you used for the purse), chain 175. Turn. Skip first chain and do a single crochet in each stitch back across chain. Chain 1, turn. Skipping first stitch, single crochet in next two, slip stitch in next stitch, chain 3, slipstitch in same stitch. Single crochet in next two, and so on, across the row. Cut thread and weave ends into the stitches. Iron flat. Pin in place to purse lining and sew to purse and frame through the purse and sew holes in the frame.

Cut chain 40". Using a split ring tool, attach purse chain ends to purse with split rings. Pliers may be needed to grip split ring as you slide it into the chain.

Finish side seams by checking to see if side seam has been sewn up to frame hinge. Secure thread by knotting and weave back into purse to hide end.

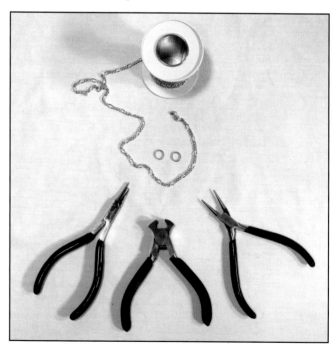

Chain tools from left: Split ring opener, chain cutter, pliers

Chapter 8: Lesson 5 – Tiny Beads
The Waterford

The Waterford is one of my favorite purses but it took more hours than almost any purse I've ever made. Between designing, stringing, knitting, framing and finishing it, it probably took over one hundred hours. But I'm proud of it. It's graphic is taken almost directly from an antique beaded purse but because the original purse was knit with the old bead knitting method, I had to re-design the whole chart to be done in new bead knitting. The purse uses size 15 beads (get your magnifying glasses ready!), size 12 Perle Cotton and size 000000 knitting needles. I didn't even know such a size existed until I researched it. Notice the mix of bead types — the water is a shimmery blue, the hills are matte and the grass is opaque. I think they work well together in this type of purse. I hope you will have fun with this. Check out some old Victorian purses online or in books and take a shot at designing one of your own based on an old pattern that you love.

The Waterford

Materials

- Size 15 seed beads — *see color chart below*
- Size 12 Perle Cotton – off white
- 2 Size 000000 knitting needles
- 5.5" Gold Square Frame (ML56)
- Gold Purse Chain
- Chain cutters
- 2 Split Rings
- Fabric for lining (pre-washed cotton/poly or satin)
- Sewing thread & needle
- Size 7 Crochet Hook

Instructions

- String rows 30–1. Cast on 86 stitches (leave a long tail to sew up side seams) and purl one row without beads.

- Next row: Knit 3 stitches, knit 80 stitches with beads, knit 3 stitches.

- Next row: Purl 3 stitches, purl 80 stitches with beads, purl 3 stitches.

- Continue with these two rows until you finish knitting row 30. String rows 60–31. Work these rows as previous rows. Finish up to row 60, then string rows 90–61. Work these rows, then string rows 118–91, and complete. After row 118, do two rows without beads and bind off. Make second side as the first.

- With right sides facing up, align both sides of purse and sew side seams using Mattress Stitch. Sew from bottom to top, and sew only up to about row 84. This is where the frame will begin. Do not fasten off thread, but leave loose in case adjustments must be made. Sew bottom seam with Perle Cotton or Nymo.

Medium Blue (sky)	*Grass Green (grass)*
Light Blue (clouds)	*Pale Green (hill)*
Tan (house shadows)	*Olive Green (bushes & trees)*
Light Brown (tree trunk)	*Medium Green (bushes & trees)*
Dark Brown (windows)	*Black (bushes & trees)*
Red (roof)	*Pink (house & flowers)*
Dark Red (roof shadows)	*Yellow (flowers)*
Caramel (field on hill)	*Off White (path)*
Lavender (hill)	*Light Gray (fence)*
Sand (hill)	*Dark Gray (fence)*
Gold (fringe)	*Sparkly Dark Blue (water)*

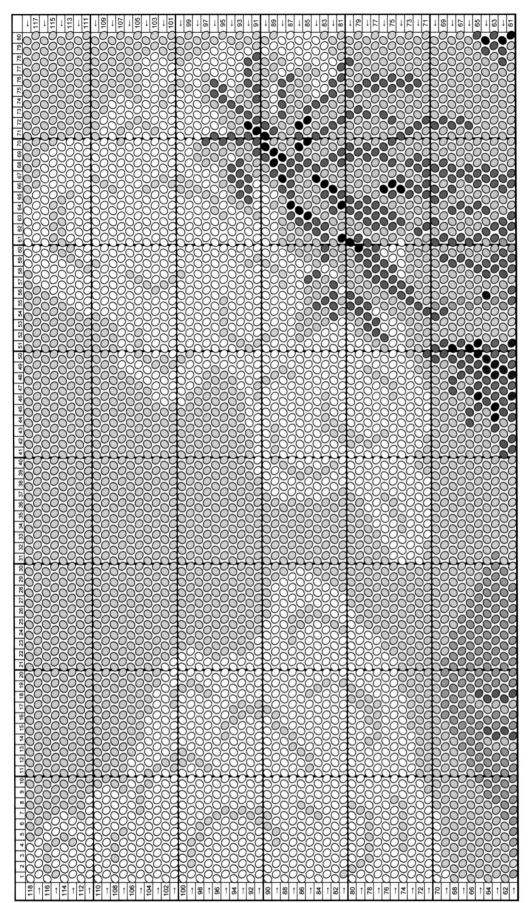

Stringing top of "The Waterford."

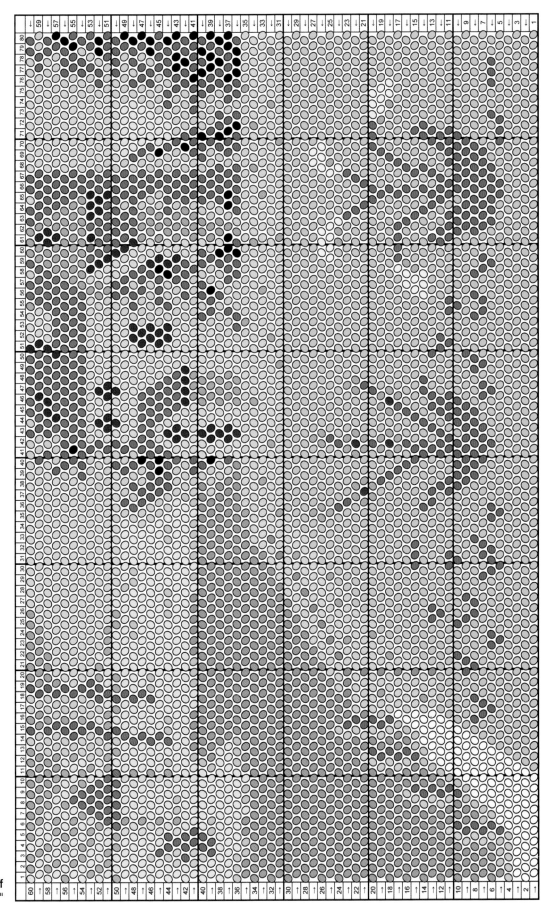

Stringing bottom of "The Waterford."

Close-up of fringe.

Fringe – Interlocked Loop Fringe

Make fringe as described on page **25** for "The Pasadena," except string 30 green beads (same color as grass), 1 gold bead, and 30 green beads for each fringe.

Lining

Make lining as described on page **39** for "The Chantilly," using the illustration for approximate dimensions.

Chain

Cut a chain about 16" long. Attach split rings to chain and to purse with split ring tool and pliers (see description on page **40**).

Finish side seams by checking to see if side seam has been sewn up to frame hinge. Secure thread by knotting and weave back into purse to hide end.

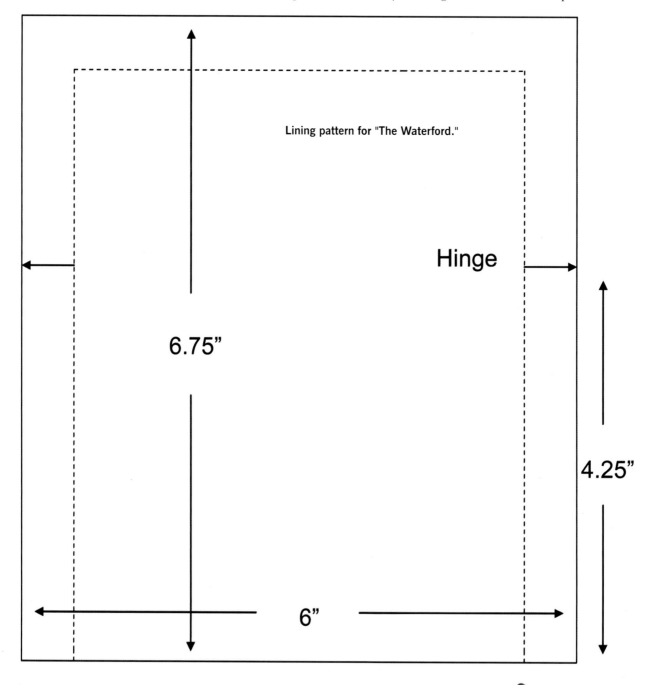

Lining pattern for "The Waterford."

Hinge

6.75"

4.25"

6"

Chapter 9: Lesson 6 – Playing with Color
The Inverness

I love plaid. I wear a lot of plaid and I have a book that shows pictures of all the Scottish Tartans. I have a plaid dress that's pretty old now, but I still love it, so I thought it would be fun to make a purse to go with it. The more I studied it, the more I learned about mixing colors. I also found that there are more colors in plaid than you might think at first, because every main color mixes with every other main color to form a secondary color. It was easy to find the main colors for this purse, but much more difficult to find the secondary colors. For example, the red-green had to be compatible with both of my specific red and green choices; the purple had to relate to both of my red and blue choices, and so on. But it was fun to study a plaid in detail and observe how the colors all crossed each other. When you look closely at any plaid pattern, it's helpful to keep in mind that the fabrics were originally (and sometimes still are) woven. The color combinations occur because one color weft thread is crossing another color warp thread. That can't be done when working with beads so we have to try to find a color that combines the two "crossing" colors.

On the chart, the red-green color combination is represented by brown; the blue-green is represented by teal and the blue-red combination is represented by purple.

Left: The dress.
Below: *The Inverness*

Materials

- Size 11 seed beads — *Green, Red, Blue, Blue-Green, Red-Green, Blue-Red, Yellow*
- 8 Perle Cotton, Dark Blue
- Gold Purse Chain
- Lightweight Interfacing (not iron-on)
- Fabric for lining (pre-washed cotton/poly or satin)
- Sewing needle and blue thread

Instructions

- String rows 37–1. Cast on 54 stitches (leave a long tail for sewing side seams) and purl one row without beads.

- Next row: Knit 2 stitches, knit 50 stitches with beads, knit 2 stitches.

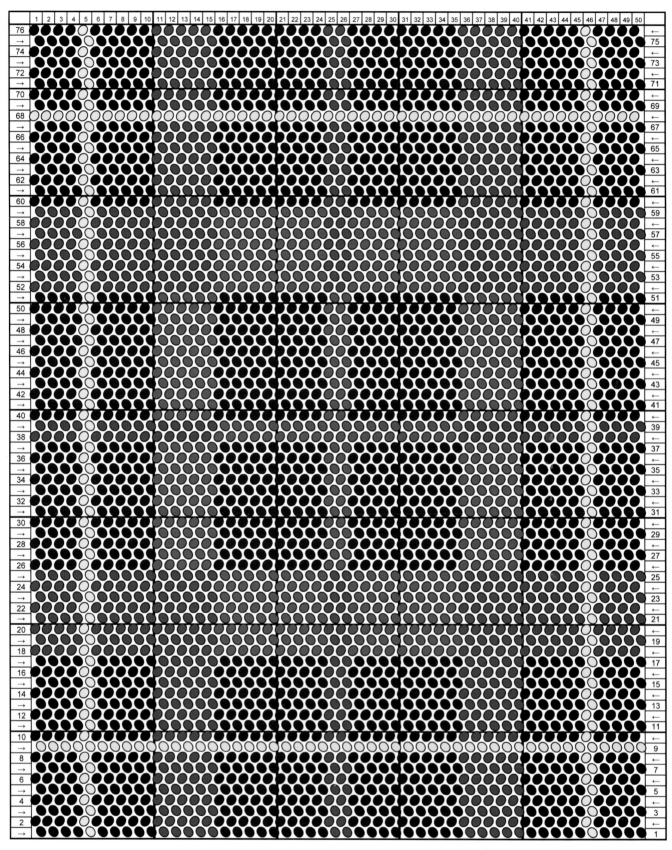

Chart for stringing "The Inverness."

Chapter Nine: Lesson 6 – Playing with Color

- Next row: Purl 2 stitches, purl 50 stitches with beads, purl 2 stitches.

- Continue with these two rows until you finish knitting row 37. String rows 76–38. Work these rows as previous rows. Bind off after row 76.

- Make second side as the first, but don't bind off after row 76. String rows 25–1, then string row 2, then row 1, again. Knit this section right on top of row 76 of side 2. After last row with beads, purl one row and knit one row. Bind off next row.

- Using Mattress Stitch, sew up side seams, being careful to match colors on back and front. On top flap, fold over unbeaded knit edges on top and sides and tack down with needle and blue thread.

Fringe – Twisted Fringe

Cut a piece of Nymo about two yards long, condition with Thread Heaven and thread it onto a beading needle. Weave Nymo into an inside seam of purse, knot it, and bring it to the outside bottom right corner. String 50 blue beads and slide beads tightly up to the bottom of the purse. To make twist, grasp thread just below the beads with left thumb and forefinger. With moistened right thumb and forefinger, twist thread about seven times, each time securing the twist with your left fingers. Thread will start twisting like a snake to the right of the beads.

The free thread must be allowed to untangle before you go further. While holding the twisted thread and beads in left hand, push twists out of the length of the rest of the thread. You may need to hold purse up high with your left hand (still grasping twisted beads and thread) to allow the thread and needle to untangle.

Secure the fringe and start the next one by stitching back into the bottom seam of purse and bringing needle back out about 1/8" from previous fringe. Secure with a knot and start the next fringe. You may have to manipulate the fringe a little to form it into a nice twist. It should twist around itself two or three times. Try to do at least 7 or 8 fringes per inch for a nice, full fringe.

Twisted Fringe: 1. String 50 beads. 2. Grasp and twist the thread. 3. Hold twist with left hand while securing fringe. 4. A finished twisted fringe.

Cut two pieces of interfacing.

Lining

To make the purse stiff enough to hang properly without draping, cut two pieces of lightweight interfacing. Cut one about 4 ¼" x 5" for the front and another about 4 ¼" x 7" for the back (your purse measurements might vary slightly). Turn purse inside out and sew interfacing directly to the purse front and back.

Measure piece of lining fabric about 14" x 5". Fold one short end over ½" to outside and baste (this will be the lining for the front of the purse.) Fold front lining up about 5 ½". Pin and sew seams from bottom fold to basted seam. Remove basting thread. Iron entire length of side seams to fold to the back. Do not sew lining into purse until chain has been inserted.

Chain

Cut a piece of chain about 4' long (length of purse along each side plus whatever length you want for a carrying chain). Sew sides of chain directly to inside of purse, along seams, starting at the bottom of the seam, all the way up to the top of the seam. Do this on each side.

Now sew the lining into the purse. Insert the lining to fit along top flap and front edge. Sew front of lining to front edge of purse. Sew back lining to fit right along sides and top of flap, folding over top edge about ½". Leave a small opening in the lining to accommodate the chain.

Sew chain to side seams; top flap is on left, body of purse is on right.

Slide the lining into purse.

Chapter Ten: Lesson 7 – Combining Knitting and Crochet
The Baltimore

The Baltimore is another one of the purses I have designed that takes a motif from an old purse. A friend got the antique purse for me from an estate sale. I have no idea of its provenance, but it's a fine example of bead knitting on a tiny scale. It is lined with satin and even has a small gathered pocket sewn in. I often wonder who made it. I would love to talk with her about technique, threads, bead sources, and patterns. Maybe I'll be able to meet her some day.

Materials

- Size 11 seed beads —
    Cream, Light Red, Medium Red, Dark Red, Light Blue, Medium Blue, Dark Blue, Light Brown, Dark Brown, Yellow, Orange, Purple, Pale Green, Light Green, Medium Green, Dark Green, Black, White
- Size 8 Perle Cotton (Off-White)
- Decorative Beads
- Size 7 Steel Crochet Hook

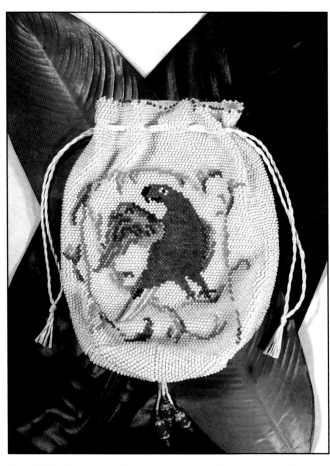

Top Right: Author's antique parrot purse. **Above:** *The Baltimore*

Instructions

- String rows 30–1. Cast on 74 stitches and purl one row without beads.

- Next row: Knit 2 stitches, knit 70 stitches with beads, knit 2 stitches.

- Next row: Purl 2 stitches, purl 70 stitches with beads, purl 2 stitches.

- Continue with these two rows until you finish knitting row 30. String rows 60–31. Work these rows as previous rows. Finish up to row 60, then string rows 94–61. Work up to and including row 83.

- Row 84: Purl without beads.

- Row 85: Knit 8, (knit 2 together, yarn over, knit 6) 8 times, knit 2 (8 eyelets made)

- Row 86: Purl without beads.

- Row 87-94: Continue knitting and purling with beads; as for body of purse, bind off. Make second side in the same way.

- With right sides facing up, align both sides of purse, sew side seams using Mattress Stitch.

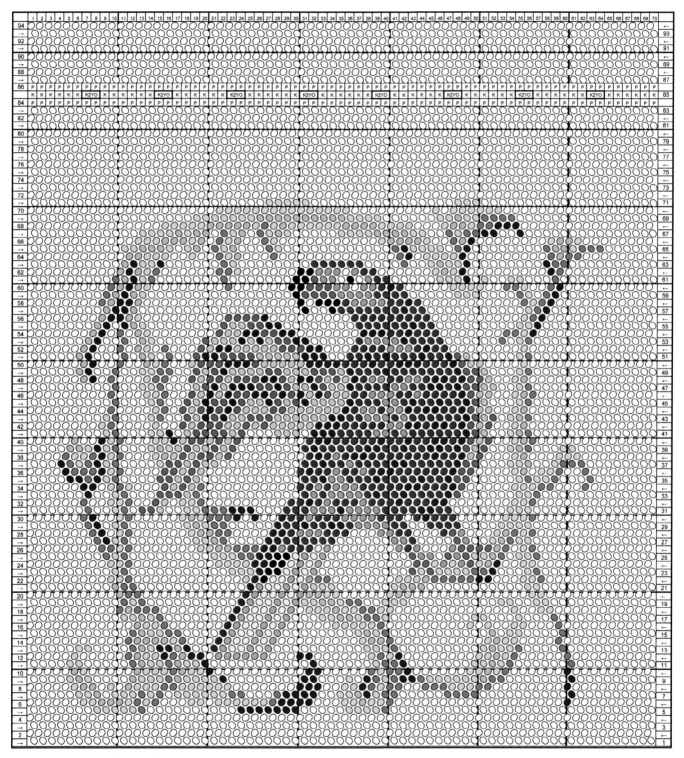

Chart for stringing "The Baltimore."

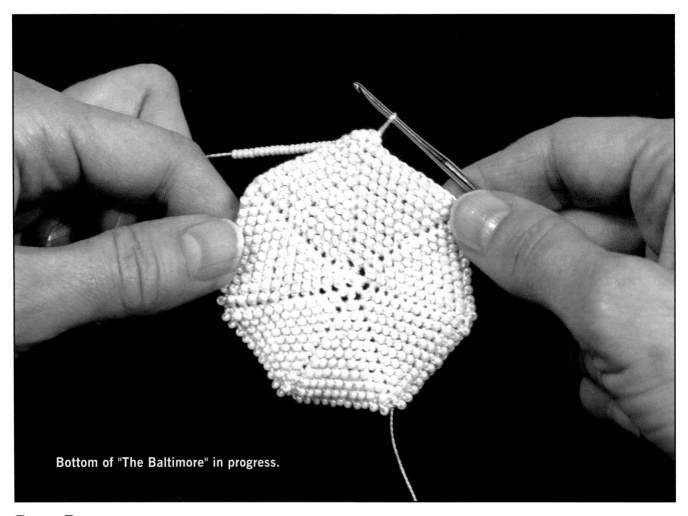

Bottom of "The Baltimore" in progress.

Purse Bottom

- String 4 strands of beads onto Perle Cotton. Chain 4 or 5 and join to form a circle. Single crochet 7 in the circle.

- Round 1: Single crochet with bead in next stitch (insert hook into single crochet in row below, slide bead up to the stitch, yarn over, draw up loop so there are 2 loops on hook, yarn over, and draw through the two loops), single crochet again (without bead) in same single crochet – Increase made. Do this around in all 7 stitches. There are 14 single crochet and 7 beads around.

- Round 2: Single crochet with bead in first single crochet, crochet with bead in 2nd single crochet, single crochet again in same single crochet (increase made). Do this for each group of 2 single crochet around. There are 21 single crochet and 14 beads around.

- Round 3: Single crochet with bead in first single crochet, single crochet with bead in 2nd single crochet, single crochet with bead in 3rd single crochet, single crochet again in same single crochet (increase made).

- Continue with rounds in this manner. There will be 7 sections of beads. You will be doing a single crochet with bead above each bead in the previous row and increasing in the last single crochet of each section. Do this for about 18 rounds. On the next 2 rounds, do a single crochet with bead in every single crochet (don't increase). You may have to do more or less rounds, depending on how loosely or tightly you knit and crochet. Hold the crochet up to the bottom of the purse and estimate how big it should be.

- Secure the last stitch of your crochet, but do not cut thread. Turn purse and purse bottom inside out and pin bottom to top. Single crochet purse bottom to purse top. Weave in all loose ends of thread throughout purse. This purse does not need to be lined.

Picot Trim

Thread beading needle with about a yard of Nymo. Weave through inside seam of purse and knot near top of purse. Bring needle to outside of purse and up through a bead on last row of purse. String one cream bead, one medium red bead, one cream bead. Bring needle back down through next bead. A picot of three beads is made. Bring needle up again through next bead in row, string three beads and go back down in next bead. Continue in this way across the top of the purse. End at side seam, weave and knot Nymo in the inside seam.

Embellish bottom of purse with several decorative beads if desired.

Drawstring

Using the same Perle Cotton as for the purse, cut four strands, each ten feet long. Fold two strands in half and tape cut ends to a table. Place your index finger through the looped end and twist the whole strand about 150 times until it gets tight on your finger. Fold the strands in half by bringing the looped end up to the taped end and at the same time, pulling the center downward. Allow the strands to loop on themselves. Remove the taped end and make a knot to secure it; make a knot at the looped end also. Repeat for the other two strands so you have two drawstrings for your purse.

Begin threading drawstring through purse from right side. Bring knotted end of drawstring through first eyelet, then out of next eyelet. Continue on around purse, going in and out of all 16 eyelets. Thread second drawstring, starting from opposite side.

Pull both drawstrings gently until the purse closes evenly. Measure about eight inches up one drawstring and make a neat knot. Make a knot on second drawstring, matching the measurement from purse. Trim drawstring about an inch up from knot.

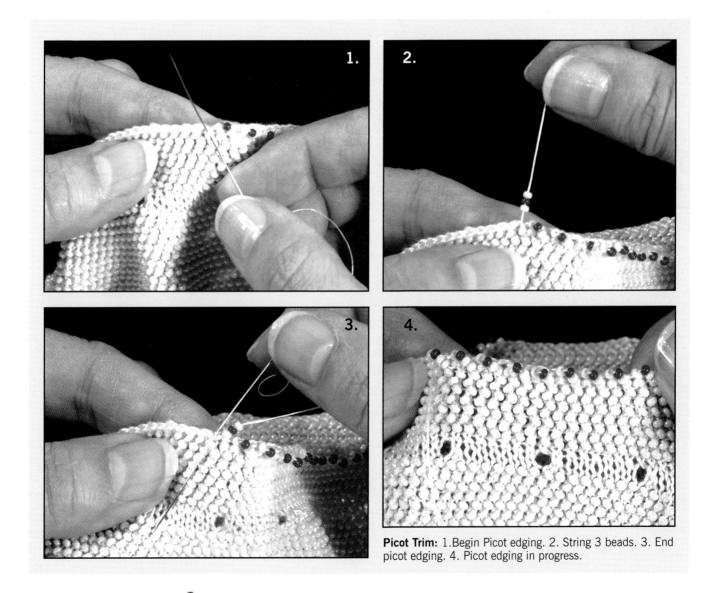

Picot Trim: 1.Begin Picot edging. 2. String 3 beads. 3. End picot edging. 4. Picot edging in progress.

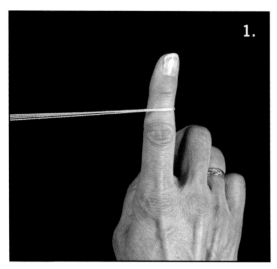

Drawstring: 1. Twist the strands with your finger through the loop. 2. Thread drawstring through eyelets. 3. A threaded drawstring.

Chapter Ten: Lesson 7 – Combining Knitting & Crochet

Chapter Eleven: Your Completed Purse

To Line or Not to Line

I have heard some pretty strong opinions on this subject; therefore I will address it. There are no rules, but there are many pros and cons on the topic of lining your purse. Vintage purse purists insist that a purse must be lined with silk or satin; others say that it's totally up to the person making the purse. I have found that whether I line or don't line really depends on the style of the purse and the purpose of the purse.

If I make a drawstring purse like "The Pasadena" or "The Baltimore," I would rather keep it unlined. A lining tends to detract from the "flow" or "suppleness" of the beadwork. Having a lining also constricts the capacity of the purse. An unlined drawstring purse hangs more beautifully. On a bead knit purse, the knitting actually acts as sort of a "self-lining." Also, if the purse is made from a Cotton Perle thread, the purse is washable.

However, adding a lining does extend the wear of the purse and keeps it from getting snagged on a fingernail or ring. It's also true that a purse with a silk or satin lining is a much more elegant looking purse. I have lined some purses with a washable cotton/poly fabric; this allows them to be cleaned easily, but still have the added durability of a lining.

A purse with a frame, such as "The Chantilly," needs to be lined. A lining gives the purse the needed stability for sewing it into a frame; and the inside looks much nicer if it's lined. A purse like "The Inverness" also needs to be lined for stability, even though it doesn't have a frame.

So, it's really up to you, the purse creator, whether you line or don't line your purses.

Caring for Your Purse

Bead knit purses are amazingly durable. They appear to be fragile, but can really take a lot of abuse. However, taking good care of your purse will prolong its life and perhaps, some day, your purse will be an heirloom!

Beads are usually color-fast, but you will find an occasional bead that is not. I found this out the hard way when I was just starting bead knitting. I gave a purse to someone who used is as part of her Victorian décor. The purse was occasionally in sunlight and, over time, the beautiful cream-colored beads turned an ugly gray. Some beads will also bleed if they are wet. To make sure this doesn't happen, test your beads in sunlight and water before using them in a purse that may be affected by these elements.

Another hazard for beaded purses is sagging. This happens more readily in beaded-knit purses, where there are swags of beads that weigh down the thread. For these purses, I would recommend that they be stored flat; only having them hang when they are being carried.

Bead-knit purses, like all the purses in this book, don't tend to sag as much as beaded-knit purses. Framed purses sag even less because of the support of the frame and lining. Most bead knit purses can be hung or carried without any problem of sagging. So if you are using these purses in décor, they can safely be hung on a wall or on a stand. But if you're storing them between uses, store them flat.

Cleaning your bead knit purse can be easy or difficult, depending on the materials used. Cotton Perle thread is washable. Purses made with this (and colorfast beads) can be hand washed. Use warm water and a little dish soap. Gently squeeze purse in suds, rinse and lay flat on a towel to dry. Purses lined with a cotton or cotton/poly fabric can also be cleaned this way. To clean other purses, bring them to a dry cleaner and ask if they can safely clean them.

Left: The effect of weight on a beaded-knit purse. **Above:** The effect of sunlight on these white beads has turned them gray.

Chapter Twelve: Basic Knitting and Crochet

Knitting

Since knitting has been done for many centuries, there have developed several different ways of accomplishing the stitches. The only common denominator is that the knitter uses two hands and two needles. The working yarn can be carried in the left or right hand, the stitch may be twisted or not, or the yarn can be brought across the right needle clockwise or counterclockwise.

> TIP: Good basic knitting instructions and videos can be found on many websites. Google "Basic Knitting."

The two most common knitting methods used in the United States are the Continental and English methods. In Continental knitting, the working yarn is carried in the left hand and easily guided around the needles. This method is a little faster than English knitting, in which the yarn is carried in the right hand and "thrown" over the needles with the right forefinger. Either method can be used for bead knitting. I am an English knitter and have been for almost forty years and I find that I can't change (or don't want to). The following instructions for basic knitting are for the English knitter. For these guides, I'm using a pair of size 8 bamboo knitting needles and Lily Sugar 'N Cream cotton yarn.

Casting On

There are, again, several methods for casting on stitches. I am showing the method I grew up with. This is an easy and basic technique, but others can be found on the web and in knitting books.

Leaving an 18" tail, make a slipknot. Place the knot on your needle and tighten, but leave it loose enough to slide back and forth. Hold the tail in your left hand and the needle in your right.

Slip knot – make a loop.

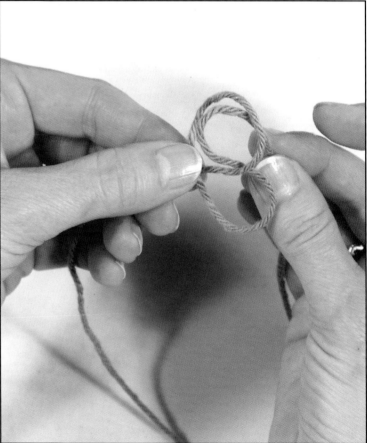

Bring a loop through the loop.

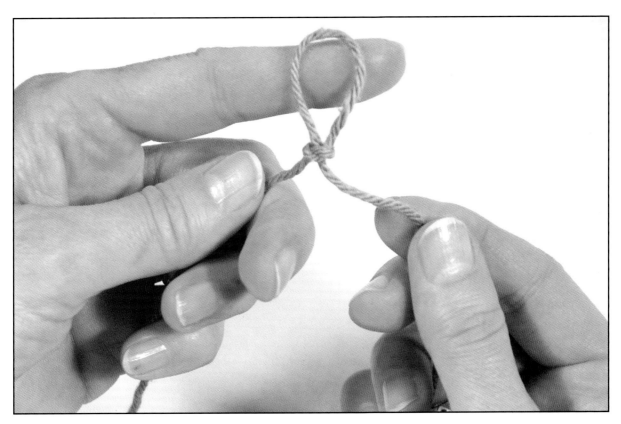

Pull the loop through the loop to form a loose slip knot.

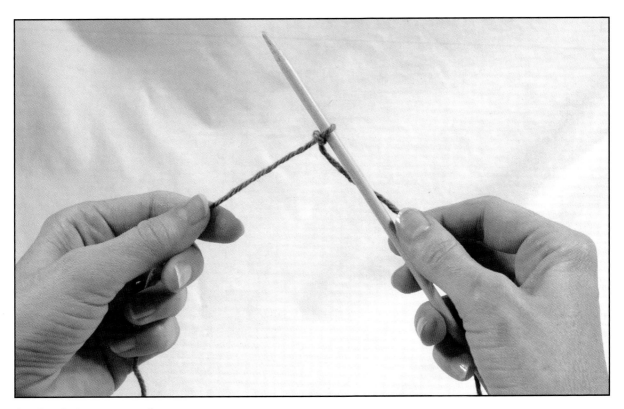

Put the slip knot on a needle.

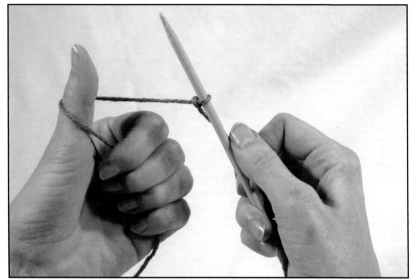

Around – hold yarn in four fingers and circle around thumb.

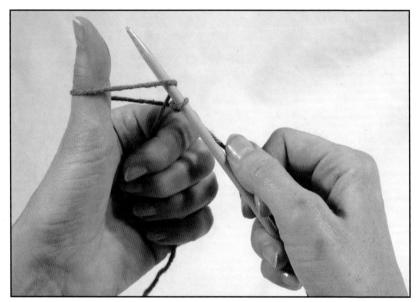

Through – bring needle up through the loop on thumb.

Circle – right hand brings yarn around needle from the back.

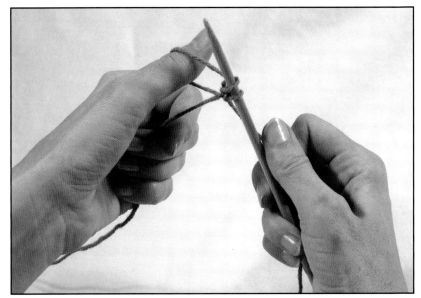

Over – bring loop on the left thumb over needle.

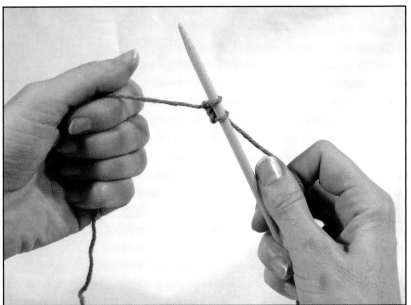

Snug – pull yarn snuggly, but not too tightly, to the needle.

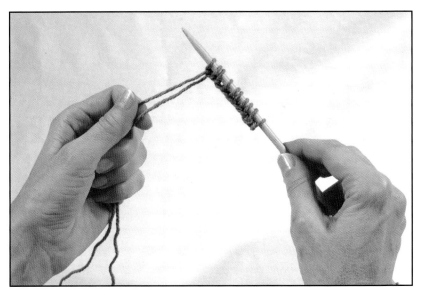

Ten cast-on stitches.

The Knit Stitch

Practice casting on until you are comfortable with it and your stitches are even. For practicing the knit stitch, cast on 20 stitches.

Practice as many knit rows as needed until you are comfortable with the knit stitch and then proceed to learning the purl stitch.

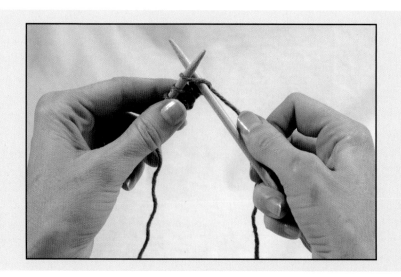

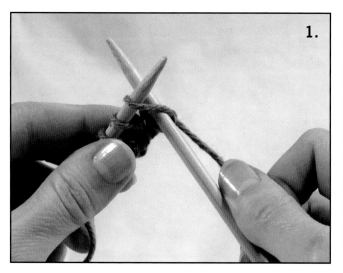

1.

In – insert needle through front leg of stitch, to back of work.

2.

Around – loop yarn around right needle from back to front (counter-clockwise).

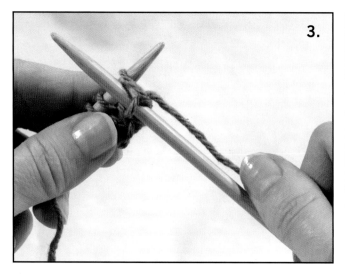

3.

Under – keeping tension on the yarn, pull new loop under the stitch on left needle.

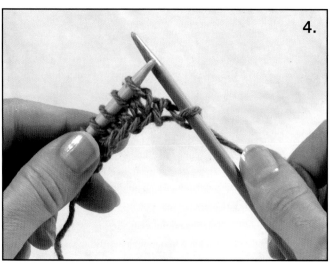

4.

Off – pull completed stitch off left needle.

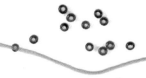

The Purl Stitch

The most common knitted objects are made by knitting one row and purling one row through the piece. This is called the "Stockinette Stitch." All the purses in this book are made this way.

In – insert needle through front leg of stitch, to front of work.

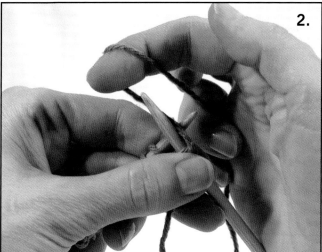

Around – loop yarn around right needle from back to front (counter-clockwise).

Under – keeping tension on the yarn, pull new loop under the stitch on left needle.

Off – pull completed stitch off left needle.

Binding Off

At the end of your finished knit piece, you'll need to bind off your stitches so your work doesn't unravel. There are several different methods of binding off — this is a common one.

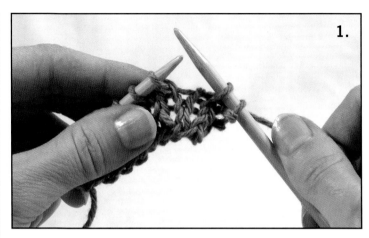

1.

Two – knit or purl two stitches (depending on if you are working on a knit or purl row).

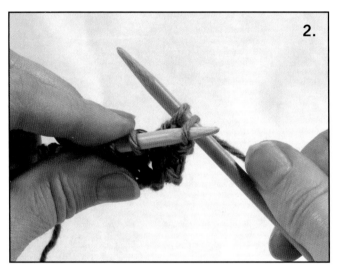

2.

Grab – insert the tip of the left needle into the first stitch (farthest to the right).

3.

Draw – draw the grabbed stitch over the other stitch and pull it off the right needle.

4.

Again – knit (or purl) another stitch and repeat grabbing and drawing.

5.

A bound-off edge.

Eyelets

For several of the purses in this book, finishing requires a drawstring. In order to make a drawstring, eyelets are required to form a "hole" through which the drawstring passes. Eyelets are easy to make. For each eyelet hole, knit 2 together, yarn over, knit 1. On the purse pattern charts, this is indicated by "K2YO." The eyelet doesn't actually show as a hole until you complete the next purl row.

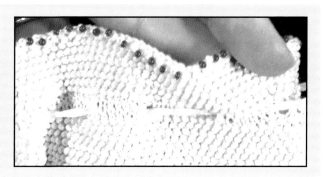

Knit two stitches together (or k2tog).

A completed "k2tog."

Yarn over from back to front.

Knit the next stitch as usual.

Last three finished stitches are K2tog, yarn over, knit 1.

Eyelets show after the next purl row.

Increasing and Decreasing

Increasing in knitting can be accomplished in two ways: you can do a yarn over, or you can knit twice into the same stitch, i.e., knit into the front of the stitch, then without removing the stitch from the left needle, knit into the back of the stitch.

Decreasing, likewise, can be accomplished in one of two ways: you can knit two stitches together, or you can knit two stitches, and then draw the first one over the second one (much like binding off).

Sewing Seams

The most common stitch to sew seams in knitting is the Mattress Stitch. Seams can be sewn in an overcast stitch or several other methods, but the mattress stitch leaves an almost invisible seam. It takes a little practice, but the effort is worth it. For the Mattress Stitch, lay the two pieces of knitted fabric side by side, right side up. Take the tail of one of the pieces and thread it into a tapestry needle. Join the other piece in the lower corner. Find the horizontal bar in each knit stitch as you go up the seam. Catch this bar with the needle on one side, then on the other side. This will draw the two pieces of fabric together and the seam will almost disappear.

Right Column - Sewing Seams: 1. Catch the horizontal bar of the knit stitch on the right-hand finished piece. 2. Catch the horizontal bar of the knit stitch on the left-hand finished piece. 3. Mattress Stitch in progress.

Crochet

Only one pattern in this book, "The Baltimore," makes use of crochet. If you're not familiar with crochet, these instructions will allow you to practice basic crochet. Only a few basic crochet stitches are taught here (chain, single crochet, and slipstitch) since they are the only stitches you'll need to know for the purse. For more crochet stitches, search the Internet or a library for basic instructions.

The Chain and Single Crochet stitches are the basic building blocks of crochet. They form the foundation for doing either flat crochet (done in a straight line) or crochet in the round (done in a circle — as in "The Baltimore").

The Chain Stitch

For this guide, I've used a size I crochet hook and Lily Sugar 'N Cream Yarn. Leaving a tail of about 6", make a slipknot and put the knot on the crochet hook. Bring yarn over the hook and catch the yarn, drawing it through the loop. Do this 9 more times, for a total of 11 chains.

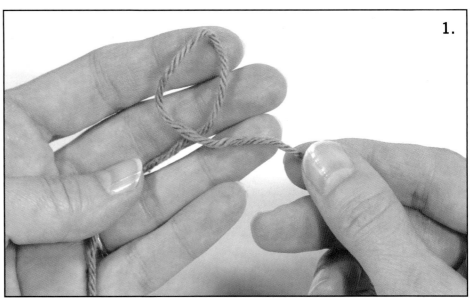

Form a loop.

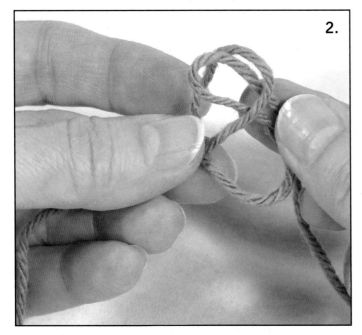

A loop through a loop.

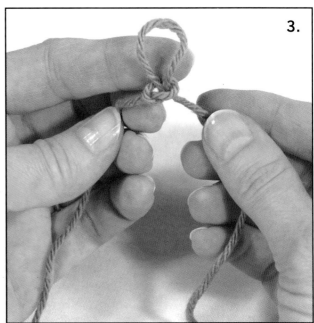

A slip knot.

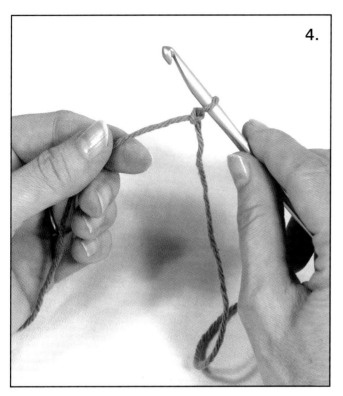

4.

Put the slip knot on a crochet hook.

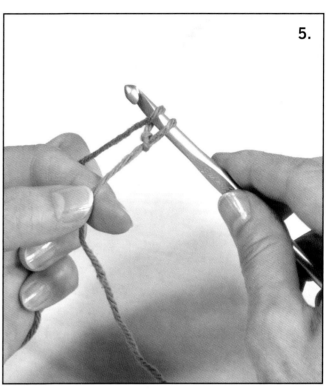

5.

Yarn over the hook.

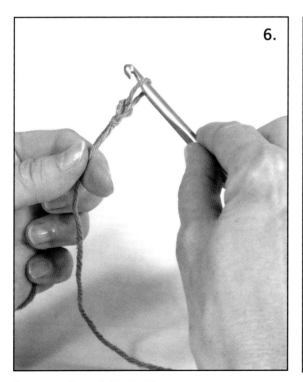

6.

Draw yarn through the first loop.

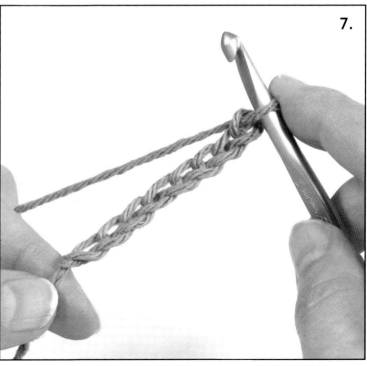

7.

A chain.

Single Crochet and Slip Stitch

Now work Single Crochet stitches back over the chain. Skip the first chain (next to the loop currently on the hook). Insert hook into the next chain, yarn over the hook and draw it through the chain. There are now two loops on the hook. Yarn over the hook again and draw through both loops on the hook. This is one single crochet. Do a single crochet in the next loop and all the rest on the chain. You'll have 10 single crochet. Chain 1 (this raises your work up to the level of the next row). Do 10 single crochet in this row. Continue in this manner until you feel comfortable with Single Crochet.

A Slip stitch is accomplished by inserting hook into the next sc, yarn over hook, and draw straight through single crochet and loop on hook (omit the second "yarn over").

Insert hook into chain.

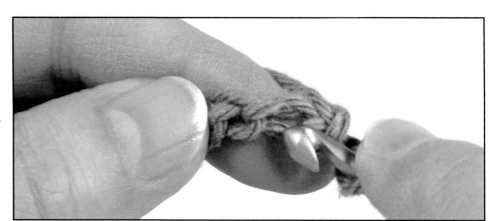

Yarn over the hook.

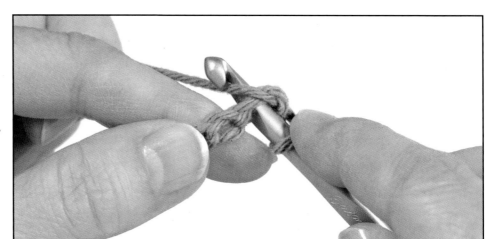

Draw loop through chain – two loops on hook.

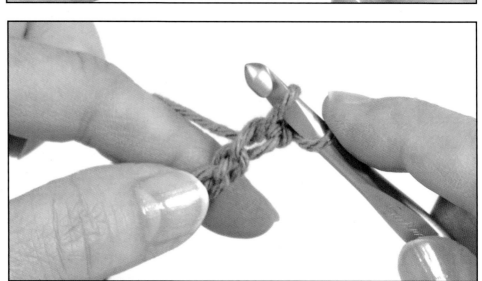

Yarn over and draw through both loops.

A completed Single Crochet.

A completed row of Single Crochet.

Do a Single Crochet into each Single Crochet of previous row.

Crochet in the Round

To begin crochet in the round, Chain 5. Join last chain to first chain with a slip stitch. Manipulate the circle so that you can see the center.

Round 1: Single crochet 7 in the center.

Round 2: Increase 1 in each single crochet by doing 2 single crochet in each single crochet (14 single crochet around).

Round 3: Single crochet in first 2 single crochet, 2 single crochet in next single crochet. Do this 6 more times (21 single crochet around). You are establishing 7 pie-shaped sections.

For the rest of the rows (as far as you want to go), in each section, single crochet in each single crochet; in the last single crochet of that section, do 2 single crochet. You will always have multiples of 7 single crochet in your rounds because you are increasing 1 single crochet in each of the 7 sections on each round.

Chain five and join to make a circle.

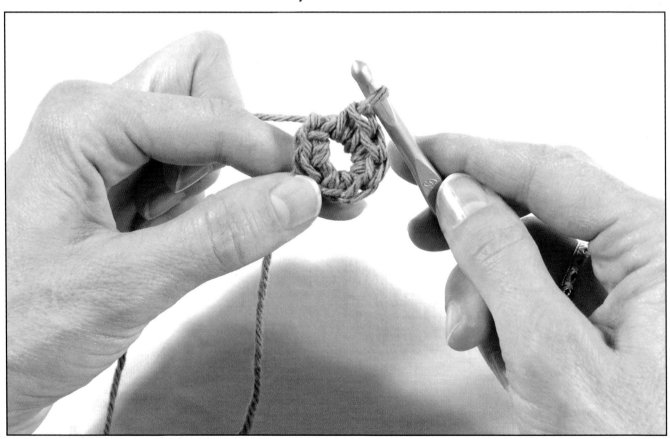

Single Crochet into the circle to do the first round.

Gallery

Design Your Own Pattern

This blank chart will allow you to play around with bead knit designs. Feel free to make photocopies for yourself, but it may not be shared or reprinted in any way. Find inspiration from old purse pictures, counted-cross stitch patterns, or just about anything that moves you. You can start your pattern by using a pencil to roughly sketch in a design, and then refine it onto other copies. You can even put a copy of the chart in your printer, print a picture onto the chart to get an idea of what it might look like as a purse, and then refine the design onto another copy of the chart with colored pencils. Designing is one of my favorite parts of creating beaded purses — have fun with it.

Materials, Sources, Suppliers

BagLady, Inc.
P.O. Box 2409,
Evergreen, CO 80437
www.baglady.com
888-222-4523
Supplies: Beads, purse frames, thread, books,
0000-000000 size bead knitting needles

Bahr Creek Llamas & Fiber Studio
N1021 Sauk Trail Road,
Cedar Grove, WI 53013
www.bahrcreek.com
920-668-6417
Supplies: Thread, bead knitting classes

Beadwrangler
228 North Sun Court,
Tampa, FL 33613
www.beadwrangler.com,
www.beadknit.com,
www.7beads.com
813-269-9257
Supplies: Beads, thread, kits,
0000-000000 size bead knitting needles

Eclectica
18900 West Bluemound Road,
Brookfield, WI 53045
www.eclecticabeads.com
262-641-0910
Supplies: Beads, thread, books

JSM Bead Coop
931 North 8th Street,
Sheboygan, WI 53081
www.jsmbeadcoop.com
920-208-2323
Supplies: Beads, books

Kralentassen
Pr. Hendrikstraat 6,
4332VS Middelburg,
The Netherlands
www.kralentassen.nl

Kralenwerk,
De Etgaarde 14,
7861 BT Oosterhesselen,
The Netherlands
www.kralenwerk.nl

Nancy Alison Custom Beaded Purses
5330 South 12th Street,
Sheboygan, WI 53081
www.nancyalison.com
920-458-4744
Supplies: Beaded purses

Out On A Whim
121 E. Cotati Avenue,
Cotati, CA 94931
www.whimbeads.com
800-232-3111
Supplies: Beads

Tri-State Antique Center
47 West Pike,
Canonsburg, PA 14317
www.tri-stateantiques.com
724-745-9116
Supplies: Antique beaded purses

Victorian Cottage Treasures
P.O. Box 753,
Porthill, ID 83853
www.victoriancottagetreasures.com
877-428-2322
Supplies: Beads, purse frames, thread,
0000-000000 size bead knitting needles

Victorian Purses by Sue
12640 South M-52,
St. Charles, MI 48655
www.victorianpursesbysue.com
989-865-6970
Supplies: Beaded knitting kits,
purse frames, thread, books,
0000-000000 size bead knitting needles

Sheboygan County Historical Museum
3110 Erie Avenue,
Sheboygan, WI 53081

Strukel Photography, Ltd.,
3615 Erie Avenue,
Sheboygan, WI 53081

Endnotes

1. Higgins, Paula and Blaser, Lori. *A Passion for Purses*. Atglen, Pennsylvania: Schiffer Publishing, Ltd., 2007
2. Thomas, Mary. *Mary Thomas's Knitting Book*. New York, New York: Dover Publications, Inc., 1938. Reprinted 1972 by special arrangement with Hodder and Stoughton, Ltd., Warwick Lane, London, E.C.A.
3. Dubin, Lois Sherr. *The History of Beads*. New York, New York: Abradale Press, Harry N. Abrams, Inc., 1998.

Bibliography

"Bead Knitting." Video. Colfax, California: Victorian Video Productions, 1995.

Belle Robinson, editor. *The Priscilla Bead Work Book*. Boston, Massachusetts: The Priscilla Publishing Company, 1912

Deeb, Margie. *The Beader's Guide to Color*. New York, New York: Watson-Guptill Publications, 2004

deJong-Kramer, E. *Classic Beaded Purse Patterns*. Berkeley, California: Lacis Publications, 1997

Dubin, Lois Sherr. *The History of Beads*. New York, New York: Abradale Press, Harry N. Abrams, Inc., 1998

Higgins, Paula and Blaser, Lori. *A Passion for Purses*. Atglen, Pennsylvania: Schiffer Publishing Ltd., 2007.

Thomas, Mary. *Mary Thomas's Knitting Book*. New York, New York: Dover Publications, Inc., 1938. Reprinted 1972 by special arrangement with Hodder and Stoughton, Ltd., Warwick Lane, London, E.C.A.

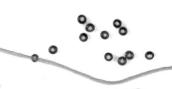